please

a field guide

don't

to creating

come

independent adults

home

(Except for a Visit)

Allyson
Hawkins Ward

Illustrated by Ron Ferdinand

Please Don't Come Home (Except for a Visit):
A Field Guide to Creating Independent Adults

ISBN-13: 978-1535426312

ISBN-13: 978-1535426312

Dedicated to my parents, Gayle Ray Hawkins and Russell W. Hawkins, who shaped my parenting skills and taught my siblings and me the importance of perseverance, integrity and hard work.

And to my children, Hattie and Kendall, who have served as my sources of inspiration.

Join the Discussion

Go to the website below to join a group of parents, grandparents, mentors and guardians who are striving to create independent young adults.

Visit this page today:

www.pleasedontcomehome.com/discussion

Contents

"We may not be able to prepare the future for our children, but we can at least prepare our children for the future."

- President Franklin D. Roosevelt

Introduction

"Coming together is a beginning; keeping together is progress; working together is success."

Henry Ford

As I stood up from tucking my three year old in her bunk bed I bumped my head on the top bunk and started to cry. I cried in part because my head hurt but I was really crying because I was scared. Less than thirty days prior I had left my husband. Our daughters and I had moved out of our beautiful home and into a small apartment. I was scared about what the future might hold for my daughters and me.

My daughters, ages three and five, jumped out of bed to hug me and looked at me worriedly as they weren't accustomed to seeing mommy cry. Of course, I didn't want to frighten them so I assured them that I would be okay, dried my tears and got them settled back into bed.

As I crawled into my own bed it sunk in that I alone would be there for my daughters and that I simply couldn't let them down. I recommitted to being a wonderful parent. A parent who would shepherd my children to adulthood in a way that would guide them to being happy, independent, successful and contributing young women.

Little did I know what a challenge that would be at the time. I assumed that since my parents had been able to do so; it must not be too difficult. How smug I was! There have been so many obstacles along the way that I never would have even considered.

In my work as a Life and Business Strategist I assist corporate management and business owners to achieve greater business success and personal fulfillment. Over the past year, more and more of my clients have begun to ask for assistance with the teenagers and young adults in their lives. They realized that the strategies I was using with my own children, like the strategies I was using to improve their businesses and lives would be valuable.

Now, more than ever, we need to empower our next generation.

There are three underlying themes to this book.

1 – We are in this together. All good parents suffer some self-doubt about preparing their children for success in life. In time we learn that a little doubt helps to make us better parents. The doubt demonstrates that we consider the challenge of rearing loving, yet independent children to be very important and worthy of our energy and best efforts. One of the most important things for you, the reader, to remember is that you are not alone. Rather, you are part of a large fraternity of very good parents.

2 – To be successful in our ever-changing world, our teens will need more than good test scores and a great GPA. While these accomplishments may help them gain acceptance to a competitive college, they do not ensure that our teens will be prepared to achieve success or happiness.

3 – Children are naturally creative, resourceful and whole. And when cultivated, these all-important traits lead to realizing the skills necessary to problem solve and transition to independence. As our teens get ready to leave our homes for college, it is paramount that our relationships with them change. The role of Supervisor served us well when they were children. As they head into adulthood, it is time for us to transition to the role of Trusted Advisor.

Today many young people are ill prepared for life after college. They have worked hard to get into the colleges of their choice. But when they get there, they either under perform, or reach out to their parents for assistance with every challenge. They don't possess the necessary skills and knowledge needed to navigate these challenges.

Consequently they find it difficult to secure a well-suited job when they graduate, and in turn, they have a tougher time getting their adult lives started.

For parents who attended college, we must acknowledge that life is very different now than when we were getting ready to head off to college. Parenting styles have changed dramatically and with this, both our ability to communicate and how we communicate with our children have evolved in a way our parents (and we) would never have been able to predict.

Can you relate to these experiences? When I was thirteen years old my brother and sister (twins) were nine. During the summers we would hop on our bikes and ride three miles, crossing major intersections, to spend our day at the town pool. Mom and dad were at work and really had no way of knowing where we were and certainly had no way to communicate with us. At the end of the day my mom would swing by the pool and spend a little time there with us. We always complained about the ride home as it was mostly uphill, but we loved our days at the pool. We spent time with our friends swimming, and just enjoying each day. We were rarely inside if it was daylight. And we didn't have the distraction of cell phones since they hadn't been invented yet. It was a simpler time.

Many parents today wouldn't dream of giving their children this level of independence. Parents are much more fearful in our 21st Century world[1]. And, it is this fear, in large part that prevents them from allowing this degree of freedom. There are too many possibilities where a child could be injured or worse: a car might hit their children; they could

---

[1] https://www.bostonglobe.com/magazine/2015/08/26/when-did-parents-get-scared/dEsGOllSt3zhFPfy1iOzKI/story.html

be abducted, attacked, or robbed. It is also unlikely that many children today would have the luxury of multiple entire days to lay about the pool with their friends. Summertime for today's young people is filled with activities. They may be studying with a tutor to improve their learning skills and ensure better grades when they return to school. They may be attending classes either for remedial help, or to get a jump on the next school year. For a promising young musician, daily lessons and/or practice can be necessary for possible entrance to Julliard or other prestigious music program. And, for an equally promising young athlete, strength and skill building, summer sports camp or other activities could be the path to a sports scholarship.

For those of us raised in the 60's and 70's, these two important factors impacted the college experience: a more relaxed parenting style and little to no technology as we know it today. When we went away to college, distance and limited communication channels separated us from our family. We had no choice but to develop our independence rather than continue to always turn to our parents.

We often had limited interaction with our parents while at school. In many dorm set-ups, there was often one phone on the hall for as many as forty students to share. And even if you could gain access to the phone there was little to no privacy. Not to forget, a long distance phone call could be very expensive, so calls were kept short. As a result, we relied upon each other or the resources of the university to resolve any problems.

We now have a powerful tool at our fingertips with Smartphones. Whether it be iPhones, Androids or other tools, they allow us consistent, and some may say constant communication. We also have the ability to find the answer to whatever question arises whether that question is related to a homework challenge or who has the fastest pizza delivery.

When my children were still toddlers my mother passed away. I had always looked to her as my strongest resource as she was a great parent. She gave her three children unconditional love. She believed in us and always supported our goals. She challenged us when she thought we could do more. She advocated for us in the classroom when she believed it was absolutely necessary. She was also a champion for all children through her work. She had earned college degree in both Early Childhood Education and Social Work. I wanted to be like her --a great parent. Having lost this invaluable resource, I became a great student taking many avenues to develop my parenting skills.

It was shortly after my mother passed away that my starter husband and I divorced. Then I was really on my own. So, I doubled down. I asked questions of people I admired, I read, I increased my skills in leadership and coaching to ensure that I reached my goal.

The truth is that we don't need a license to have children and there is no class in high school that trains us to be great parents. But there are resources out there. We just need to be focused on the desired outcome and look around for valuable guidance.

It is my goal to share the expertise I have discovered and developed with a larger audience.

This book will give you some simple guidelines to ensure that you can accomplish the final step in helping your teenage sons and daughters to stand on their own two feet by the time they finish college.

I have focused on describing and discussing the four keys needed to propel your teens to independence. Each section includes stories to illustrate specific examples of what has been helpful to other parents. There is also a corresponding website where you can access the tools mentioned within these pages.

I am honored to be on this journey with you. By investing your time in reading this book I know that you have the ability to greatly improve your teenagers' chances of success and happiness in life. I know because it is clear that you are committed.

Dependence→College→Independence

1
Unique Challenges For This Generation

"We were of the minds, 'let teachers do what teachers do.' We were out saving the world. We came when you wanted us to come."

Marie Infinito, Parent of teenagers in the 70's and 80's.

In May 2014 17 percent of college graduates did not have a job lined up when they graduated[2,3]. Wow! That's a scary number. Where do you suppose most of those young people went to live when they graduated? A good guess would be back home with their parents.

Each generation is classified into a group determined by a span of years within which they were born. There are differing views on the classifications depending upon the source. The Baby Boomers[4] are the generation that was born following World War II, generally from 1946 up to 1964. Generation X[5], commonly abbreviated to Gen X, is the generation born after the Western Post–World War II baby boom with birth dates ranging from the early 1960s to the early 1980s.

Millennials (or Generation Y[6]) are those born from the1980's to 2000. The next Generation has been referred to as Generation Z although this name has not been as widely adapted as the Millennials name. Generational study being more art than science, there is considerable dispute about the definition of Generation Z. Demographers place its beginning anywhere from the early '90s to the mid-2000s.

So, why are these generational labels of any consequence? "Each generation has different likes, dislikes, and attributes. They have had collective experiences as they aged and therefore have similar ideals. A person's birth date may not

[2] http://employer.aftercollege.com/83-college-students-dont-job-lined-graduation/
[3] https://www.washingtonpost.com/news/grade-point/wp/2015/01/30/more-than-4-out-of-5-students-graduate-without-a-job-how-could-colleges-change-that/
[4] Brandon, Emily. "The Youngest Baby Boomers Turn 50". *US News & World Report*. Retrieved 11 November 2015.
[5] William Strauss and Neil Howe (1991). *Generations*. New York, NY: Harper Perennial. p. 318. ISBN 0-688-11912-3.
[6] (Gen y) Millennial generation the next big thing By Peter W. Singer

always be indicative of their generational characteristics, but as a common group they have similarities."

There are many similarities and differences between the Millennials and Generation Z relative to previous generations (Baby Boomers and Generation X). One of the biggest differences between the two generations is technology. Millennials have lived in a somewhat digital world from early childhood; iPods and MySpace defined their teenage years. But Generation Z is the first generation to be raised in the era of Smartphones. And, many do not remember a time before social media.

This book is directed to parents of Generation Z, but with the oldest members of this cohort barely out of high school this book will rely upon various information and some studies about Millennials in the work place as an indicator of what we can expect from Generation Z as they start to enter the workforce.

The natural communication style of Millennials and Generation Z is very different than that of Baby Boomers. The biggest driver is that this group of people grew up using smart phone technology, improved computers and tablets. Here are some traits unique to Millennials.

- Visit your local coffee shop and you will find it filled with people sitting together and ignoring each other as they text on their Smartphones.
- Many don't know how to maintain eye contact.
- They often don't know how to properly shake your hand.
- The older segment of Millennials aren't interested in attending their class reunions because they know what everyone is doing via Instagram or another social media platform.

- Doorbells? What are they? They text when they arrive.
- Landline? Some have never seen one in their own homes.
- At rock concerts instead of holding up a lighter people hold up cell phones.
- When they see an accident, their first instinct is to record the moment and then post it to YouTube rather than come to someone's aid.

While these are stereotypes of an entire generation, actual human communication among Millennials is extremely limited. But, as with most bad news there is some good news.

Because so few Millennials know how to communicate, it makes those who do know how to have a real conversation stand out. The same thing may be said about a strong work ethic. Millennials are not known for their work effort, but that simply means that those that do demonstrate this as a strength will be the few and the proud that succeed.

American sociologist Kathleen Shaputis labeled Millennials as "the boomerang generation or Peter Pan generation, because of their perceived tendency for delaying some rites of passage into adulthood for longer periods than most generations before them. These labels were also in reference to a trend toward Millennials living with their parents for longer periods than previous generations."

How Things Have Changed

There are many contributing factors that have created today's college bound teens, but there are two that seem to have the greatest impact: parenting styles and Smartphone communications.

Perhaps you've heard the term helicopter parent. This parenting style is characterized by a helicopter-like tendency to hover over children with laser-like focus and swoop in to rescue them at the first sign of trouble. While many of us may bristle at being labeled a helicopter parent, if you are among the highly educated middle class or wealthier segment of society, with social and financial resources to share with adult children, it is likely to be an accurate descriptor.

On the next pages is a chart detailing some characteristics of helicopter parents. The purpose of including this is to present a clear definition and understanding of some of the characteristics of helicopter parents. You may find that some of these describe you to a T and others are counter to your parenting style.

Parenting Exercise:
Helicopter Parents

As you read the traits of helicopter parents, assess your own parenting style. Assign a number between 0 and 5 for each trait-5 being a trait that absolutely describes you. If a trait is completely opposite to your thoughts on parenting, assign that trait a score of 0.

Trait	Defined	Score
Fear of dire consequences	If my child doesn't make the team or gets a low grade there will be a disastrous consequence that could result in not getting into the 'right' college. If *I just help him/her to get through this (i.e. write the paper, call the teacher or coach) then he/she will succeed and all will be back on track.*	

Trait	Defined	Score
Feelings of anxiety	In our modern world some parents live with an elevated level of fear. They live with fears from the uncertain economy to a fear that a stranger will abduct their child. "All I have to do is know where my child is at all times and know every person with whom he/she interacts and all will be okay."	
Overcompensation	Some parents attempt to over compensate for their own childhood feelings of being unloved or neglected. "My mom was too strict. I am going to be a better parent than my mom or dad. I will be super involved with my kids AND be their best friend."	
Focus on what they feel they can control	This generation has more single heads of household than the generation in which we were raised. Parents will often pour themselves into a relationship in which they think they have more control. As the child succeeds the parents take the success as a direct reflection of themselves. *"My kid is my best friend. I don't need a romantic relationship filled with uncertainty. I feel great when I see my kid excel among his/her peers."*	

Trait	Defined	Score
Focus on what they feel they can control	This generation has more single heads of household than the generation in which we were raised. Parents will often pour themselves into a relationship in which they think they have more control. As the child succeeds the parents take the success as a direct reflection of themselves. *"My kid is my best friend. I don't need a romantic relationship filled with uncertainty. I feel great when I see my kid excel among his/her peers."*	
Peer pressure from other parents	In some circles parenting has become a competition with opposing teams. Competing teams can vary, including such match-ups as stay at home parents vs. working parents resulting in many judgments lobbed against someone from the other team. This constant judgment of other parents creates even more pressure to produce a 'successful child.' *Susan's kid got an award at school that we (my child) missed out on. What extra activity can we add that will ensure we (my child) wins next time?*	

How did you fare? If you scored a 25 please send me your address so I can send you a propeller hat. Just kidding, there is no need to bury your head in shame. Just notice where you might fit in on a spectrum of parenting styles with helicopter on one end. The truth is that there are many drivers as to why we are able to focus more attention on our children than our parents were able to. The question becomes, what is the impact of all this attention we are focusing on our children?

> *"Failure and challenges teach kids new skills, and, most importantly, teach kids that they can handle failure and challenges."*
>
> *Dr. Deborah Gilboa, MD, Parenting and Youth Development Expert*

In a discussion with one of my coaching clients the client lamented, "I don't remember it ever being my parents concern about whether or not my siblings and I were happy." Perhaps you can relate to this thought. When I was growing up and a girlfriend and I got into an argument, our parents did not intercede. If I scored poorly on a test my mother never considered calling the teacher to complain or help me to get assistance. She looked me squarely in the eye and told me I had better remedy the situation and… "Oh by the way, you can forget going out with your friends on Friday night." In other words, it was a problem that I had to solve on my own.

With some clarity around the typical actions of a helicopter parent, let's examine the impact it can have on the children.

Impact of a Helicopter Parent on Kids

Decreased confidence and self-esteem.	The message read by our children when parents intercede is that my parents don't trust me to do this on my own. This leads to a lack of confidence.
Under developed coping skills	With parents cleaning up or preventing any challenges and roadblocks that come their children's way, the child loses the opportunity to learn to cope with disappointment or failure.
Increased anxiety	A study from the University of Mary Washington has shown that over parenting is associated with higher levels of child anxiety and depression.
Sense of entitlement	Children who have always had their social, academic, and athletic lives adjusted by their parents to best fit their individual needs can become accustomed to always having their way, thus they develop a sense of entitlement.
Under developed life skills.	Parents who always tie shoes, clear plates, pack lunches, launder clothes, and monitor school progress, even after children are mentally and physically capable of doing the task, prevent their children from mastering these skills themselves. Additionally, they rob the child of the pride of accomplishing these tasks and building upon them

What is the specific impact of these phenomena on your college bound teen?

In her article 5 Signs You Were Raised By Helicopter Parents Huffington Post Senior Healthy Living Editor Anna Amendrala writes, "While hovering may have a positive intent it can have a negative impact. College counselors across the nation are reporting higher rates of general anxiety in this generation's students. And kids who say they had over-controlling parents have higher levels of depression and report feeling less satisfied with family life. When they receive parental support that they didn't ask for, they feel less competent and have less initiative than peers who weren't parented in this way, and thus, they lack a sense of confidence because of it."

She further points out "While most parents start scaling back their involvement when children head to college, helicopter parents tend to ramp up support. The worst examples of helicopter parenting include previously unheard-of behaviors like parents attending their adult children's job interviews or calling college professors to argue over a grade. "

At this point you are likely to be thinking one of the following thoughts.

Option 1: You are shaking your head and saying this is crazy! I would never call my child's college professor or employer. Great. Keep reading. The advice in this book will guide you on how to help your teens stand out as they transition from college to the real world.

Option 2: What do you mean? Of course, I am going to call my child's college professor or employer if they are being treated unfairly. Great. Keep reading. The advice in this book will guide you on how to help your teens stand out as they transition from college to the real world.

Option 3: Hmm....I don't plan to call the school but there could be an extenuating circumstance that I am uniquely qualified to explain to the professor. I don't see any problem with that. Great. Keep reading. The advice in this book will guide you on how to help your teens stand out as they transition from college to the real world.

Bye-Bye Big Bad AT&T

A major external influence that separates our teens' experiences in growing up from ours would have to be the telecommunications industry. Based upon the lawsuit brought by the United States Department of Justice on January 8, 1982, AT&T Corporation relinquished control of the Bell Operating Companies that had provided local telephone service in the United States and Canada up until that time[7].

As a result there were two things that contributed to significantly lower long distance prices. For the first time, there was competition for your business from such companies as Sprint and MCI[8]. And, secondly, prior to the breakup, AT&T had increased the cost of long distance service to offset the burden of providing local service that

---

[7] Frum, David (2000). How We Got Here: The '70s. New York, New York: Basic Books. p. 327. ISBN 0-465-04195-7.
[8] Tunstall, Brooke (1985). Disconnecting Parties: Managing the Bell System Break-Up, an Inside View. New York: McGraw-Hill. ISBN 9780070654341

was much less profitable. Now thirty years later we can call across the country for no more than a local phone call. And most Smartphone plans today include free unlimited local and long distance phone calls in the monthly fee.

In 1993 when my first child was born, my husband was working about a one-hour commute from where we lived. To ensure that I would be able to easily alert him when I was in labor, and that he had better head to the hospital, we got him a 'baby pager'. The baby pager was just like any other pager but with a shorter contract and the sole purpose of alerting dad to the arrival of the new baby.

Just ten years later in 2003, 70 out of 100 people had a cell phone. The reason for the increase in cell phone usage was the reduced cost of service brought on by competition. Additionally, there were multiple manufacturers making cell phones. This combined with the increased demand caused a drop in the price of cell phones, making them accessible to more people.

In early 2007, Apple Inc. introduced the iPhone. The iPhone was one of the first Smartphones to use a multi-touch interface[9]. What made the iPhone such a big hit was its large touch screen and that you could use your finger instead of a keyboard or stylus. Shortly thereafter, the first phone to use Android was released. The ease of use and competition helped to rapidly take over the market of dumb phones.

The combination of a move towards helicopter parenting and the opportunity for increased communication has had a significant impact on our children.

---

[9] http://www.applegazette.com/feature/6-things-apple-did-not-invent/

Assuming that parenting styles are not likely to change soon, and that the immediate communication between parents and children now provided by technology is here to stay, we need new strategies to help our teens not only graduate from college but also to enter into happy and successful self-sufficiency. Therefore, now is the time for us to transition to the role of Trusted Advisor.

What is a Trusted Advisor?

In business the trusted advisor is the role that sales people and consultants most want to attain with their customers. They wish to be considered a partner with the customer. But not just a partner, rather they want to become a trusted resource for the customer.

Some of the attributes of Trusted Advisors include:

Term	In Business	In Parenting
Transparent	Integrity and honesty are key.	This is particularly important as they meet and learn to trust new friends and resources. They will turn to a Trusted Advisor as a person from whom they can count on honesty.
Focused on the Client's Success	Brings insights and resources to the client's business.	An opportunity to support students in their goals that may or may not be the same as those of the Trusted Advisor.

Term	In Business	In Parenting
Straight Talkers:	Are open and honest	Beyond honesty, a Trusted Advisor is willing to have the tough conversations. This relationship is different from one with a peer who might be unwilling or unable to be open.
Support Network	Have affiliations and networks that they can tap into not directly available to the client.	Open their networks to aid the student in identifying internships, jobs, or career counseling.
Respectful	Will listen to the client and genuinely want to help without doing the work	By listening and not solving challenges for them, a Trusted Advisor respects that teens are naturally creative, resourceful and able to solve their own challenges.
Reliable	They do what they say	A Trusted Advisor follows through on any commitments.

A number of people may serve as Trusted Advisors to your student. I am hoping that you can see what an important role this is for all students and work to serve in this capacity for your child. This role is different from that of a Supervisor. A parent in the role of Trusted Advisor will guide his/her child at their request rather than demand that they follow a parent's direction.

25

The transition starts in high school about the time they get a driver's license. With a driver's license comes increased responsibility and freedom. When my daughters obtained their driver's licenses I started to release the reins a bit. When they would inquire, "Mom, can I....?" My reply was, "I don't know, can you...? My objective was for them to consider what other obligations they had and whether or not they could do whatever they requested. They would consider their other obligations and then we would have a chat about how they would proceed. It was a stepping stone on the way from my role of Supervisor to Trusted Advisor.

My daughter, Hattie, developed a relationship with several women with whom I know through a social organization. There is Carla, with whom she formed a particularly close relationship. This woman is an attorney, a profession Hattie plans to pursue. There are also other things about this woman that my daughter admires. Over time they have formed an enjoyable relationship and Carla serves as a mentor to my daughter.

My other daughter Kendall has interests that run to more creative pursuits. When she was thirteen a close friend of her father was able to arrange a photo shoot in New York City. At the time Kendall wanted to be an actress and having a headshot and other modeling shots was what she most desired. This woman, who works as a fashion model, has taken an interest in my child and has used her network to help my daughter achieve her initial goals.

I firmly believe that "it takes a village to raise a child." I have looked on favorably, with oversight, when others have supported my children. If you are fortunate there will be many people who will take an interest in your children and extend beyond your skills and network to expose them to new ideas, opportunities and people. It is less likely that they will serve as a Trusted Advisor, as they won't make the same level of investment in your child, but they will be great mentors.

At the writing of this book I am planning a trip to my daughter's college as she finishes her freshman year. She was one of a handful of freshmen to land an internship this summer. I have mixed emotions about this. I am very proud of her initiative and focus on getting this internship. And at the same time, I hate that my baby isn't coming home this summer to live with me.

Part of me wants to take the credit for her good fortune. I did point out the importance of securing an internship, although I also suggested pursuing one as a freshman would be a lofty goal. The truth is that this is a kid who has been focused and goal oriented for some time. In 7th grade she borrowed the book of courses offered at the high school she would be attending, and mapped out her four years of coursework over the weekend. She is an excellent communicator, respectful to her elders and just basically presents well. As a result, whenever she has needed assistance securing internships or introductions to people who could assist her she has had a network of people happy to help her through the process.

It's too early to determine if ten years from now this child will be the most successful of her classmates, but it is certain that when she does receive her B.A she will have a well-defined idea of the type of work she wants to do. Whether she loves the work or hates the work, she will be a step closer to selecting a path that advances her goals. Additionally, she will also have a leg up against the competition next summer when she is seeking another internship. She will be able to build upon this real work experience to successfully compete against her classmates who do not have the same level of experience.

In years past, college graduates often had the opportunity to join the company at which mom or dad had worked for twenty-five years or more. This option is seldom if ever available to students today. Many parents have been downsized-- and in addition to possible downsizing, the secure income of a hefty pension that previous generations benefited from does not exist today.

With the writings of Thomas L. Friedman, author of The World is Flat, in mind, we should be acutely aware that those living locally are not the only ones competing for opportunities in our own backyard. Many years ago people lived their whole lives in one neighborhood. Today we are willing to move for the best opportunity. And, any technologist can explain to you how many jobs that were once held in the United States are now filled in India.

The purpose of this book is twofold. First is to help us navigate to a new relationship with our children. As discussed, to best help our children succeed, we, as parents, need to move from the role of Supervisor to that of Trusted Advisor. Second, although it is unlikely that we can impact the statistics showing that only 17 percent have a job lined up when they graduate, it is our job as Trusted Advisors to give unfair advantage to our clients--our kids, to ensure that they are part of the 17 percent.

A comment about the low percentage of graduates who have secured employment by graduation day: there were a number of different studies all of which showed different percentages. Because each of the studies[10] touted a lower percentage than we might expect (each certainly under 40 percent), for the purpose of this discussion, I just picked one and went with it. More important than comparing the numbers reported by various studies is recognizing that a large number of students graduate from college and go long periods attempting to secure meaningful employment.

As a single mom I've often felt that I and I alone was responsible for guiding and providing for my children. While I was convinced that divorcing the children's father was best for me, I was also committed to ensuring that this decision in no way prevented my girls from being equipped to succeed in life. My definition of success was that I raise children who know how to make themselves happy, are able to provide for themselves at whatever financial level they desire, make a contribution to the world and have choices in life.

---

[10] http://time.com/money/3857107/college-graduates-career-ready-overconfident/

2

Setting a New Standard

"I am still learning."

Michaelangelo

I remember after first getting divorced that I was scared. How was I going to parent these two incredible gifts I had been given to become happy, confident young women who would contribute to society? My mom had passed away so I called the next best person I knew, my aunt—my mother's older sister. When I laid out my misgivings to her about not having a partner to share my concerns about raising my children she shared her own story.

My uncle was a Marine and the family had been stationed in Japan. Sometimes he would be out on assignment for months and she was on base at home with three little girls thousands of miles away from her family. She, too, had been afraid. "How am I going to do this on my own?" she worried. She held a belief that she needed her husband's input, counsel and support to succeed at raising their children. Her circumstance caused her to reexamine her beliefs. Then she realized that my uncle had never given much input to raising the girls, even when he was there. So there really was no difference with him being there or not.

As I reflected on her story it made me realize just how similar our situations were. The truth was that my former husband fell into a similar category. He did not provide much input. In fact, what input he provided was of little value. He placed a much lesser value on parenting than I did.

I recall a conversation we had once. He shared that his own father was not a great role model. In his mind all he had to do was exceed his father's level. So if his father got a score of two on a scale of 0-10 and he upped his game to receive a score of three then he was satisfied. Since I was trying to figure out how to score a ten in parenting, we were really at odds. Often times his input was not thoughtful and usually was at odds with the goal. In fact, after we were divorced I now had the ability to parent without a negative influence. Once I realized that, a huge weight was removed and I was excited by the opportunity.

Before I had children I was at lunch one day with a colleague and one of our vendors. The vendor, Karen, was sharing her frustration with her three-year-old son. Each night when the child went to bed Karen or her husband was required to lay on the floor next to his crib until he fell asleep or the child would throw a tantrum. Naturally, this would result in them falling asleep on the floor and waking in the middle of the night from a pain in the back. I found this story very disturbing. Although I didn't yet have children, I knew for sure I had no intention of sleeping on the floor in my child's room for three years.

What outcomes can be anticipated from this act?
- The child learns early on that tears can manipulate his/her parent (s). Instead of the parents being in charge, the child is in charge.
- With this pattern established early on, there is a greater likelihood that the dynamic of whether the parent or the child is making decisions will remain skewed to the child. This will make it much more difficult for parents to provide the increased direction needed as the child transitions to toddler and teen-age years.
- This prevents the child from developing and pursuing behavior patterns that serve as pathways to independent choices.

- What is the impact on life and marital relations?
- The stress from the lack of sleep was certain to inject ongoing frustration into their day-to-day lives.

- The ongoing sleep deprivation was likely to negatively impact each partner's level of performance in daily responsibilities including work, childcare, and interpersonal relationships.
- The consistent need for at least one parent to sleep on the floor interfered with and in time could have caused a rift in the couple's relationship.
- The parents were likely jeopardizing their own health and/or well being by sleeping on the floor night after night.

Karen might have actually been frustrated about the lack of resourcefulness she and her husband were able to muster up, as well as their willingness to allow their child to so negatively impact their marriage.

My Resources

I knew that I would need new resources since I was without my number one resource, my mother. Luckily, in addition to my aunt, there were numerous resources available in the form of books, videos, seminars, etc. I began my journey then to uncover all of the resources I could to help me be a fantastic parent.

Reading

A few years after seeing Karen's predicament, I had my first child. Because I definitely did not want to replicate Karen's experience I read several books on how to lovingly and effectively put your child to sleep. I put what the experts suggested into place and by the age of three months my daughter was in bed at 8:00 PM every night without ceremony. I recall friends being over to dinner one night and they couldn't believe that it took me only ten minutes to walk upstairs and put my girl into bed and return to my guests for adult time.

Some time later I went to visit a dear friend who had recently had her first baby. As we were chatting she said it was time for Ava to go to sleep and she clothed her in her pajamas and then proceeded to rock her to sleep with me there. I questioned this and she described for me her process which sometimes worked and sometimes didn't. She confided that she was frustrated and missed having time with her husband in the evening because of this nighttime ritual.

Fortunately, for both of us I had already established myself in our circle of friends as a resource for thoroughly researching and deploying child rearing strategies that worked. I shared the method I had learned via the books I had read and applied with my first child. At first she was reluctant because she didn't think her husband would like the approach as it allowed for the baby to cry for a little while. But she was desperate and she trusted me, so she decided on a plan to initiate the process when she knew her husband would be away on business for a few days.

Two weeks later I received a card in the mail thanking me for my guidance and sharing how happy she was that it worked. She went on to say that she was much less tired and she and her husband had reclaimed a couple of hours each evening to spend together.

Seminars

I've spent tens of thousands of dollars on seminars of various varieties to develop skills. Reading to learn is great, but I found that when you find the right environment, in-person training dramatically reduces the time to learn. It also offers the added benefit of developing a community of like-minded people to call upon as resources.

Leadership Training

Somewhere along my journey I decided that I wanted to know how to lead others in improving their careers and personal lives, and also to be better able to guide my children. I pursued several avenues, including leadership training and neuro-linguistic programming training to improve my skills.

The benefits of my training have been multi-faceted. In my corporate role I can walk into a room and confidently assess the situation and offer suggestions and/or take control of the room if there is a lack of leadership present.

Both of my girls have served confidently as leaders in their teams and clubs. And when they are confronted with a new challenge they will often seek my counsel on how they might more effectively achieve their desired outcome.

Coaching

In 2004 I had the good fortune to have my first experience with coaching. I purchased a package that included three seminars and three months of coaching. My coach helped me stay focused on what was most important. If you are like me, sometimes even though we know what's most important, we get off track. The other thing the coach helped me to do is see the blind spots. Blind spots are the things you can't see or don't recognize, which are keeping you from accomplishing your goals. Blind spots can be things that are missing or things that don't belong. Blind spots can be hidden anywhere — in your mission, vision, strategies, process, behaviors, attitudes or beliefs. Even someone as talented as award-winning golfer Tiger Woods has a coach to aid his efforts to excel to even greater levels.

Sometimes I am questioned as to how coaching is different from therapy. The way I sum it up is that a therapist looks back over what is causing a challenge and a coach looks forward and helps you to hone your gifts so as to improve your ability to take advantage of opportunities.

Since my initial three-month trial, I have hired a number of different coaches who have helped me realize opportunities in many facets of my life. They have kept me on track and served as sounding boards on specific projects. They have also helped to more clearly define problems and then, with a clear definition encouraged me to find a solution. Another great benefit of working with a coach is being able to draw upon the coach's ability to point to beliefs that may be limiting success. They do this by asking probing, well-targeted questions that point the way to useful responses.

In time, I found myself simultaneously benefiting from a coach and developing my own coaching skills through books, course work and finally completing my coaching coursework and serving my own clients.

Over the years I have had the opportunity to aid a number of clients who, in the course of other coaching, have presented with challenges as they relate to their children. We have worked to repair relationships with their children and provide them with specific tools to prepare their children for success. To follow are a couple of specific stories which you might find useful.

Samantha was struggling with her daughter Claire, a college graduate, who had failed to launch. When she graduated college, she was one of the lucky ones to secure a position working in her chosen field. However, on the personal side, she continued to act like a child/student dependent upon her parents. She showed no signs of moving into her own apartment. She was not contributing financially to the household; nor was she doing any of the housework. Much like when she was a teenager, she expected that meals be prepared for her and she never took the initiative to clean the kitchen after meals.

Samantha and I worked together to get to the root cause of what was really going on. Samantha realized that she had created a monster because of her guilt over a messy divorce. She had been compensating by paying bills and cleaning for the young woman. She understood that what she had been doing to 'help' her daughter had actually done more harm. The daughter didn't know how to take care of basic things required in her own home because she had never been required to do so. Using the same skills you will find in this book, we came up with a plan for Samantha to get things back on track and create a timeline for her daughter to move out. This eased her emotional stress and fear that she was letting her daughter down, and it allowed her to guide her daughter through a successful transition to a new, adult life in her own home.

Craig had recently been divorced and his daughter, Madison, had cut off all communication with him while she was still in high school. As she approached leaving for college, he was increasingly worried that he would not have the opportunity to influence or advise her in this next stage of life. Together we dissected what was really going on. When Dad had moved out of the house, Madison felt abandoned and did not want to be vulnerable to someone she couldn't rely on, so she cut off all communication.

Understanding this as the background to the current situation, we developed a strategy for resuming communication through a focused effort to ensure his consistent presence in her daily life. Sometimes this was as unimposing as daily texts that went unanswered. His consistency paid off! And as he embarked on his new relationship with his daughter, Craig was now able to use the skills in this book to coach Madison to independence as she headed off to college.

3
GRIT

"I've always believed that if you put in the work, the results will come."

   Michael Jordan, Basketball Legend

"If you want to become the world's number one investor, there is no substitute for hard work."

   Warren Buffett, The World's Most Successful Investor[11]

"There are no secrets to success. It is the result of preparation, hard work and learning from failure."

   Colin Powell, Former US Secretary of State,
   US Army 4 Star General and Chairmen of the Joint Chiefs
   of Staff

---

[11] *Incademy Investor Education*. Harriman House Ltd. Retrieved 20 November 2015.

S uccess leaves clues. You can look at any number of successful people and see the paths they have taken to reach and, at times, exceed their goals. In the following chapters you will find the four primary lessons practiced by successful people, customized to help your teen navigate his/her way into a successful adulthood. These four keys have been defined to help you not only understand them but also to use them to guide your teen to independence. You will also find additional support on the web (www.pleasedontcomehome.com) to guide you in helping your teen to transition smoothly into adulthood.

I've chosen the word GRIT as it represents the building blocks for seeing your teen through to become an independent young adult. It serves as a reminder that, in most cases, a solid, focused effort is what is required to achieve success. GRIT also stands for:

Game Plan
Resourcefulness
Investment
Transformation

Everyone doesn't get a prize – American Idol Auditions

Have you ever watched American Idol? When my girls were younger (ages four and six) we started watching the show together. There were some very talented vocalists. At other times, we would watch and be amazed that certain Idol hopefuls would have the nerve to go on national television and embarrass themselves. Note, I'm not referring to the attention-seekers with little or no talent who were downright awful—and knew it. They were there for the opportunity to be so bad that they would get the attention they craved. There were plenty of other young people who had no talent and were genuinely surprised when the judges told them as much.

The question my children would ask is "don't they have any friends?" What a great question from children so young. It seemed like these would-be stars didn't have anyone to tell them honestly that they simply didn't have talent. We felt bad for them. How horrible—and embarrassing—it was to have someone finally speak honestly and to have that message delivered in front of millions of people. Often times the lead judge, Simon Cowell, would say, "it's better for you to know now at this young age so that you can put your efforts into something else." The truth is that while his feedback seemed harsh it was a gift.

At some point in time it was decided (consciously or unconsciously) that our children's egos would be crushed if we didn't praise, acknowledge and reward them-warranted or not. For those that grew up in the 70's and 80's this wasn't true, yet we saw some of the greatest innovations and business growth in history at that time. Just take a look at the dot com boom. Only those people with unique ideas and a strong work effort or GRIT rose to the top and stayed there.

In the 90's there was a shift in parenting to the idea that we needed to reward every child and every effort-- often for little more than showing up, lest their feelings would be hurt, or they would be discouraged and scarred for life. The practice began wherein every participant received medals and trophies simply for participating in sporting events and academic competitions. In my own county I witnessed this many times as the 7th, 8th and 9th place 'winners' were called to the podium to be recognized. This is not how it works in the real world, so why give kids false expectations? No one seemed to consider what would happen to these young people when they left the nest and suddenly didn't get so much as an 'attaboy' from their manager for simply showing up to their jobs.

Many people consider Michael Jordan the greatest basketball player of all time. What made him so great? Even at the height of his success, in addition to the workouts that he and his team mates did regularly, he spent more time in the gym lifting weights to further improve his strength and in turn, his skills.

A complaint I often hear from business owners is that one of their biggest challenges is employees who want all of the rewards and recognition, but are reluctant to put in the extra time and effort it takes to excel—and stand out. Hard work is necessary whatever the pursuit. Rightfully or wrongfully deserved, Millennials have the reputation of being lazy. So your teens are entering the workforce with that label attached to them.

Think about your own success in life. What was required to get to where you are today? We can look around us and find many examples, regardless of the field, of people who have been willing to work hard to succeed. This is true of teachers, nurses, engineers, athletes and most other professions. In most cases, those that have worked the hardest are typically the people at the top of their pyramid. There are no shortcuts for reaching the top.

Employers Lament: Help Wanted...Any Takers?

According to the evening news, many people are out of work and finding it difficult to secure jobs. And yet I also hear from business owners and company managers that they cannot find qualified people to fill their open positions. Two specific occasions stand out during which I heard specific complaints regarding a lack of employable young people to fill jobs-- one from a small business owner and one from a manager at NASA.

My friends own a heating and cooling company. The 'techs' earn up to $100,000 annually. While college is not a requirement, technical skills and training are, and finding qualified people to fill these roles is a challenge. Until recently, not everyone felt compelled to attend college, or at least give it a try. They pursued other career paths after high school. The trades were one of the more popular career paths. People would attend trade school and then, if they were fortunate, apprentice with an established tradesman (plumber, electrician, etc.). After putting in their time they might establish their own business. What is different today is the emphasis on attending college. In many communities pursuit of anything other than a four-year college career,

45

such as attending trade school, is frowned upon. This shift has made it more challenging to find skilled trades people to hire.

A client of mine is a manager at NASA. He shared with me just how difficult it is to find teenagers for the agency's open internships for high school students. His challenge in filling these positions surprised me, as it seems to me that working at NASA would be a dream place to work if you were interested in any of the various disciplines in which it offers internships. I asked him why he thinks so few students seem interested. His reply was that the kids don't appear to want to do the necessary work to:

- Identify the opportunities that interest them;
- Create a resume and apply; and
- Do the required work once they get the job.

And finally, they are not ready to make the possible sacrifices in other areas of their lives like missing out on social events. That conversation really left me shaking my head.

I am not making the case that Millennials are lazy. Actually, they may well work hard, but they have the expectation that opportunities will find them, not vice versa; and that they will be rewarded and praised consistently along the way. As life will generally not meet their expectations, they will likely experience a degree of discontent with any position, resulting in a lot of job-hopping.

What Prevents Our Young Adults From Achieving Success?

In addition to a lack of GRIT, limiting beliefs can also hold our teens back from emerging as successful young adults. Limiting beliefs are those that disempower us in some way; in believing them, we do not think, do or say the things that they inhibit.

We have beliefs about rights, duties, abilities, permissions and so on. Limiting beliefs are often related to our self-identity. Limiting beliefs may also be about other people and the world in general.

There are two reasons that limiting beliefs are harmful. The first reason is that they contain a presupposition that nothing will change in the future. Saying you're not good with money leaves no room for change, it is what it is and you're stuck.

The second reason they are harmful is that when you say or think something like you aren't good with money, your brain sorts for evidence to support the belief and it will nearly always find the support by remembering times when you felt that you weren't good with money and ignoring any evidence to the contrary.

Then you create a self-fulfilling prophecy as you carry on 'knowing' you're not good with money.

A self-limiting belief will always have some element in it that suggests things cannot and will not change. Look for more about specific limiting beliefs in the chapters ahead.

Am I Prepared To Guide My Teen?

If you are feeling a little apprehensive as to whether or not you are comfortable moving into this new role of Trusted Advisor with your teen, I empathize with you. I harbored a range of concerns when I began the process with my daughter. What I found was, by following the steps laid out for me by various experts with whom I consulted, I was able to achieve great success in realizing my objective.

Specific Concerns

I don't want/believe I can do it (psychology)	Eek! I don't know if I have the skills to guide my child through the four keys in this book. I don't have the mastery in some of these areas myself. --That's okay. There is nothing wrong with you learning and applying some of these skills yourself. In fact, if you haven't mastered a skill this is a great time to be vulnerable with your teen and let them know that you are working to improve yourself as well. This will go a long way in developing your relationship and setting a positive example for your child. He/she will also get the added benefit of understanding that learning is a life long pursuit.

Specific Concerns (continued)

Don't have a mentor (me)	How can I do this on my own? The good news is you don't have to. I have invested a good deal of time, money and effort into seeking information, sorting through for the best answers and methods, asking questions -- and learning how best to guide my daughters! And now I have poured the best of what I learned into this book. And I will be here to assist you via this book, the website, individual coaching, or a group training/coaching.
Don't have a big enough reason why I need/want to do it.	Consider this scenario. It's graduation day from the school that you have just invested more than $100,000 into and your young adult is moving home with you. He/she has no job and what's worse, no plan. He/she has moved into your basement and has increased your food bill and electric bill because while you are out every day working he/she is at home sitting on the couch watching TV and/or playing video games. Act now or pay later!
There's just not enough Time	I don't have time to do this: I have another teen/other children at home, I have a full time job, I am a single parent, I have a part time job in addition to my full time job. Use your N-E-T to get it accomplished. N-E-T stands for No Extra Time. That means when you are commuting to work, or walking on the treadmill or cooking dinner listen to an mp3 or a podcast on your area of interest.

Throughout the book you will find boxes highlighting **Chief Talk**. These are the little nuggets that my father, Russell, shared with me as I was growing up. When he was in his 30's he was given the nickname, The Chief.

While I learned a great deal about parenting from my mother, it was my father who guided my siblings and me on financial issues and resiliency in life. One of his favorite things to say when we faced a challenge was, "you have to keep getting up." That may or may not have a big impact on you but when I was in college and as a young adult I could hear his words in my head whenever I faced a challenge and was propelled to take action.

4

Game Plan

In the book Alice in Wonderland *there is a scene:*

"Alice asked the Cheshire Cat, who was sitting in a tree,
'What road do I take?'
The cat asked, "Where do you want to go?"
"I don't know," Alice answered.
"Then," said the cat, "it really doesn't matter, does it?"

Lewis Carroll
Alice's Adventures in Wonderland

The first component of GRIT is G for Game Plan – a plan for you and your teen. There are four elements to a game plan. These include vision for where your teen is headed, a roadmap for how to get there, the stepping stones they will use and setting their expectations as to how you, as parent, will support your teen's vision. But before we get into these elements it is important to understand why you and your teen need to have a game plan.

Imagine if someone approached you and said I have a wonderful opportunity for you to invest $100,000. Wow, you might think –sounds like it must be a great opportunity to require such a large investment. Most investors would want to know what they can expect to get in return, when they would get it and the likelihood that what is being promised will happen. If the answer is, *"Well, maybe you will get a tenfold return or maybe you will get the opportunity to continue to pour more money into the project for another ten years, we don't know the odds of success."* What the heck?! No one would take that business deal! But many parents take that deal every day when they fund their children's college education.

If you are a parent who is planning to contribute all or part of the cost of your child's college education, it's important to understand what you are investing in. The truth is that college, whether it is private or public, is a tremendous investment of money and time. As parents we may need to decide whether we should invest in a child's college education or in our own retirement. Based upon your age, financial position and other factors, your Financial Advisor may suggest that paying for your child's college education is not a wise choice for you. Since I am not a Financial Advisor I can't comment on that. What I would recommend is that you have a conversation with your child to understand why he/she is planning to attend college and what outcome is expected after this four-year investment of time and money.

This book is focused on addressing parents whose children have decided to attend college. However, it is important to note that college isn't for everyone. There are many other wonderful opportunities available including the military and trade schools. The practical ideas in this book may be of assistance regardless of the path your child chooses.

If you have ever baked a cake you started with the final product (vision/goal) in mind. Once you have your vision or cake in mind you choose a recipe and then gather the required ingredients to make the cake. The recipe is your roadmap and the ingredients are the stepping-stones on your roadmap to achieve your vision.

There are times in this book when the word goal is used in place of vision. A vision is an activated goal. Its description is richer and more vivid.

Parent Exercise:

1. Write down anything in your life that was once a goal, dream or desire. Be sure to add to this list those things that seemed impossible to achieve.

2. Put a star next to two or three items that were the most difficult to achieve.

3. For the two or three items you have starred, write down the steps you took to achieve this goal. Did you focus on it continuously? Did you have an emotional commitment to the goal? Did you create a vision? Did you create a roadmap to get there? What were the steps you took to achieve your goal?

The intent of this exercise is to put you in touch with your own process of goal setting to remind you just what you can achieve through goal setting and a focused effort. As you guide your student to create goals as part of a larger game plan, you can reference your own experience and have examples ready to call upon.

Vision

Step one is defining your vision. Often times people admit that even if they don't know exactly what they want to do, they have a pretty clear picture of what they don't want to do. That's a start! But to avoid ending up on the wrong path, it's always better to start with a vision of what you do want. You will find this to be much more powerful. Remember that this vision for what your student wants isn't set in stone.

Here is a list of elements that may be used to help your student develop a vision:

- Geography – Where does your student want to live? What part of the country or what country? Does he/she want to live in a city, suburban or rural area?
- Next steps? Are these pre-determined as in the case of law, medical or professorship careers?
- Field of Interest – Is your son or daughter interested in pursuing a career in advertising, healthcare or the financial industry?
- Income – What type of salary does he/she want to earn?
- Office/Field – Is sitting in an office or being out and moving around more ideal?
- Customer Interaction – would your teen prefer to interact with customers/clients or not?
- Collaboration – Does he/she like to collaborate or work independently?
- Employee/Business Owner – does your child aspire to work for himself or herself or as an employee at a small, medium or large company?
- Impact – what impact, if any, does this young person want to have on his/her community?

Each of these considerations and many others are valuable as your teen decides what an ideal lifestyle is for her/him. The other thing to consider when creating a vision of the future is to know why he/she wants it. This may seem like an inconsequential question but it is worth consideration.

If your student has no idea what his/her vision is, one way to get started is for you to ask her/him to think of someone he/she admires or who has an interesting job. Encourage your student to interview that person (or read about him/her) and determine what the requirements are to achieve the same goal. Naturally, as he/she moves along an education path and gains more experience your student might decide that the original vision just wasn't right. There is still benefit in setting off with a vision as it improves our chances that we will take action and work hard at pursuing that vision.

Giving Your Vision Power

As teens develop their vision, it is important for them to be clear on why this vision is important to them.

Imagine you are standing on the top floor of a fifty-story building. You look across to a matching building and you can see the tightrope that has been strung across and connects the two. The sun is shining and the birds are flying by. If you were offered $100 to walk from one building to the next with no safety net below your reply would likely be a resounding "NO." "My mama didn't raise a fool!"

What if, however, the person you most love in the world was sleepwalking across this tightrope and appeared to be paused and teetering in the middle? Would you say yes to getting across the tightrope? Most likely you would walk, crawl or quickly determine another way to reach that person and bring him/her to safety.

What's the difference in the two scenarios? The difference is that your WHY is different. $100 is not a motivator, but saving the person you most love evokes a different response. In the second scenario you wouldn't be thinking about personal risk or how you would do it. You would just be focused on getting it done—and done right!

So what does all this have to do with your teen's vision for college and after? Committing to college and what lies ahead is a big goal. Along his/her path there may be many obstacles including:

- a challenging professor,
- a troublesome roommate,
- many social opportunities,
- limited finances,
- a change of interest
- and others, whether they be personal, educational, professional, recreational, et.al.

We all want to help our children avoid the pitfalls, and by advising them to be sure this is what they want we increase their chances of success. If a student isn't passionate about the "why" of this investment in time and energy, he/she is more likely to fall off the path. One way to help your student examine the "why" is through the use of a simple analogy: the "why" is like the bumper guards in bumper bowling. The guards are there to help the player stay on track with the game plan of getting the bowling ball to the pins at the end of the lane. The "why," therefore, serves to help the student avoid veering off course in her/his pursuit of fulfilling a defined vision.

The Value of an Internship

According to a survey by *The Chronicle* of Higher Education and *American Public Media's Marketplace,* employers want new graduates to have real-world experience. Internships and work during college matter most: Employers stated that each of these was about four times as important as college reputation, which they rated least important. Relevance of coursework and grade-point average rounded out the bottom of the list.

Roadmap

Now that your student (with your help) has formulated a vision (yippee!)-- is he/she on the right path? Step 2 in formulating a game plan is the roadmap.

For every goal there are many paths a person can take to achievement. Be sure to consider some traditional steps like specific coursework and some non-traditional steps that may provide reinforcement or additional "skills" such as clubs, on-campus work-study, and summer employment. Also help your student think through what relationships might help to improve the chances of successfully achieving his/her ultimate goal. Later in this chapter you will find specific examples of some of these steps.

Ask your student to answer the following:
What are some of the requirements?
- Grades – Does your vision require maintaining a specific grade point average?

- Internships – Are there summer internships that will make you more attractive to a potential employer? Have you investigated what it would take to get one of these internships?
- Language – would proficiency in a language improve your chances of success?
- Are there other steps—academic, extracurricular or outside of school—that would improve your chances of reaching this vision? If so, list them and note how you could pursue these steps.

What other resources can you call upon to reach your vision?
- Recommendations – will you need recommendations from your professors to get into your next school, or job?
- Network – what type of people can aid you in getting an introduction to an employer or admissions director?

Finally, be sure to reinforce with your student that he/she need not worry about making sure that every step along the path is right…the key to getting to a personal vision is taking action, imperfect or otherwise.

Stepping Stones

Once your student has a vision in mind and has started to develop a roadmap, it's time for step three. Identify the stepping stones that will help in reaching his/her vision. These stepping stones will come in the form of smaller goals. This is a way to chunk down a bigger objective into bite-sized pieces. Let's use a student who plans on a legal career as an example. We'll call the student Amelia. If

Amelia's vision is to gain access to a competitive law school there are a number of items for her to complete:

- Gain clarity on what is required to gain admission –
    - Is there a required GPA?
    - Are letters of recommendation required?
        - Who would be the best candidates to write recommendations?
    - What courses will best prepare Amelia for advanced coursework?
    - Are there insights about the school or the admissions process that would help Amelia to be better positioned for admission?
        - Who does Amelia know who has attended the target law school?
    - What internship will best prepare Amelia for a career in law?

Identify specific stepping stones (small goals) that will get Amelia closer to the vision. To accomplish this advise Amelia to make an exhaustive list for each of these steps. Advise her to write down any and all possible avenues to address the list above. There is always more than one way to accomplish a goal and with an exhaustive list if she hits a roadblock, she can simply try another path.

One stepping stone might be securing letters of recommendation.

Once a list of steps has been identified, you will want Amelia to define several SMART goals (stepping stones) for each semester.
S – Specific
M – Measurable
A – Attainable

R – Relevant
T – Time specific

Examples of SMART goals for every student
pursuing a similar path as Amelia are:

- *I will identify 3 people in (or through) my extended network who attended xyz law school, schedule and complete a 30 minute interview with each of them by the end of the semester.*
- *I will identify a professor who is the best person to write my law school letter of recommendation, I will develop a short list of 3-4 possible choices by the end of the semester using all resources available to me.*

This is where your role as Trusted Advisor comes in. This may be the first time that, like Amelia, your student has tackled a goal setting exercise like this. It is appropriate for you to offer guidance or simply to be a sounding board in helping him/her to figure out what the stepping stones are. Once the stepping stones are in place it is important to check in regularly as you both move forward to make sure progress toward reaching these goals is on track.

Your role is not to manage the process but to offer to be an accountability partner for your student. An accountability partner's job is to hold the person accountable as defined by the source requesting accountability. Studies have shown that when we declare our goals to someone else and commit to accomplishing them we increase the likelihood that they will be completed.

If your student thinks this would be valuable, have her/him pick two check-in dates about five weeks apart for a status of her/his progress. Notice I didn't say if you think this would be valuable. You are a Trusted Advisor and not a Supervisor so it should be your student driving this and not you. It is important to ask the following questions

- Have you accomplished the goal? If the answer is yes, or partially— remember to celebrate!
- Are you on track to accomplish the goal? If yes, celebrate!
- Does the process you are following to accomplish the goal need to be tweaked?
- Do you need to take greater action to meet the goal?
- Is there some way that I can support you in reaching this goal? This is not your chance to do the work for them to reach their goals. Rather this is your opportunity to provide resources if needed and requested.

Setting Expectations

The fourth step in this process is to set expectations for both you and your child. This will help you both to avoid future upsets about how you will support her/him in college. The topics in the following chart may seem basic, or not all that critical. But, each will, at least in part, require your continued investment of resources, including time and money. Depending upon your situation they may conflict with other things that require these resources. Being clear on how you plan to offer ongoing support in each of these areas and then communicating this to your student will benefit all. By setting realistic expectations you and your student will eliminate or reduce conflict. Some of the things your child will want to be clear about are:

Financial	What, if any, financial support will your student receive from family? Will this include tuition in addition to an allowance? Will he/she be expected to cover part of the expenses via scholarships? Loans? Work-study?
Emotional	When your student leaves home, how much/often can he/she expect communication from you and other family members? Will you make it to parents' weekend, sporting events, etc?
Rules for returning home over semester and summer breaks	Will there be a curfew while at home? Will your student be expected to work over the summer? Will he/she be expected to help care for younger siblings? Will visits from college friends be welcome?
Network	Are you able and willing to make introductions on your student's behalf to increase possible summer job opportunities? Job opportunities following graduation?
Ongoing	How will the levels of support change from year to year? What if your student opts for immediate graduate school after 4 years?

In the chart regarding setting expectations, we discussed emotional support, of which communication is an important support element. When Bruce was leading a large team while working for a large American corporation in Japan, his son John attended high school in Japan. When it was time for John to attend college, he had to make a decision between attending college in Japan or returning to the United States. This was before Skype and other tools, so his decision included considering possible limits on the communication between father and son. This was one of the things that John had to take into consideration when choosing his preferred college. He opted to return to the United States. Because he did consider it in advance he was less bothered that his parents weren't able to make his college basketball games like those of his teammates. Setting expectations for less *emotional support* in advance and putting other support systems in place avoided heightened disappointment that might have negatively impacted John's college experience.

Putting It All Together

Here is an example of a 4-year vision and roadmap for a student who plans to attend a top tier law school.

Student's Name:
Vision: Attend and graduate from a top law school following the completion of my undergraduate degree.

- o Freshman year –
    - Study a variety of topics to expose myself to possible majors.
    - Make the Dean's List

- o Summer –
    - Return home to live and connect with my family.

- Work to earn as much money as possible for my Sophomore year.

o Sophomore Year –
  - Complete entry-level required common core college courses
  - Make the Dean's List
  - Declare a major.

o Summer –
  - Internship
  - Start looking at possible law schools that will meet my objectives.

o Junior Year –
  - Enjoy the courses in my major
  - Study abroad to gain foreign language proficiency
  - Complete cores as necessary and maintain a A-/B+ GPA

o Summer –
  - Internship
  - LSAT prep

o Senior Year –
  - Enjoy my major classes; take the LSAT

o Summer –
  - Travel internationally and practice language skills

o Post Grad – Enter law school in the Fall after College graduation.

Tip! : Be sure to encourage your teen to establish a LinkedIn account to start networking now. LinkedIn is the leading business networking site and the quickest way to extend your reach when you are looking to expand your network. See www.pleasedontcomehome.com for 6 things for your student to keep in mind when creating a LinkedIn profile.

5

Resourcefulness

"Success is not about your resources. It's about how resourceful you are with what you have."

Tony Robbins
Life and Business Strategist

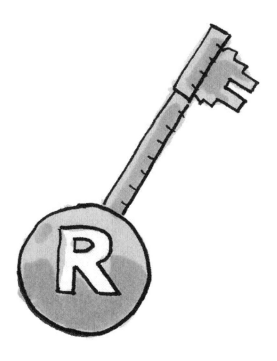

The Red Paper Clip Guy[12]

- On July 14, 2005, he went to Vancouver and traded the paperclip for a fish-shaped pen.
- He then traded the pen the same day for a hand-sculpted doorknob from Seattle, Washington.
- On July 25, 2005, he travelled to Amherst, Massachusetts, with a friend to trade the doorknob for a Coleman camp stove (with fuel).
- On September 24, 2005, he went to California, and traded the camp stove for a Honda generator.
- On November 16, 2005, he made a second (and successful) attempt (after having the generator confiscated by the New York City Fire Department) in Maspeth, Queens, to trade the generator for an

---

[12] Red Paper Clip Guy - "Man turns paper clip into house". BBC News. July 11, 2006

"instant party": an empty keg, an IOU for filling the keg with the beer of the holder's choice, and a neon Budweiser sign.

- On December 8, 2005, he traded the "instant party" to Quebec comedian and radio personality Michel Barrette for one Ski-doo snowmobile.
- Within a week of that, he traded the snowmobile for a two-person trip to Yahk, British Columbia, in February 2006.
- On or about January 7, 2006, he traded the second spot on the Yahk trip for a cube shaped van.
- On or about February 22, 2006, he traded the cube shaped van for a recording contract with Metalworks in Mississauga, Ontario.
- On or about April 11, 2006, he traded the recording contract to Jody Gnant for a year's rent in Phoenix, Arizona.
- On or about April 26, 2006, he traded the one year's rent in Phoenix, Arizona, for one afternoon with Alice Cooper.
- On or about May 26, 2006, he traded the one afternoon with Alice Cooper for a KISS motorized snow globe.
- On or about June 2, 2006, he traded the KISS motorized snow globe to Corbin Bernsen for a role in the film Donna on Demand.
- On or about July 5, 2006, he traded the movie role for a two-story farmhouse in Kipling, Saskatchewan.

So what does this true story about Kyle MacDonald[13], the Red Paper Clip Guy have to do with the success of your student in college? By solving all of their problems for them, today's parents are depriving their children of the

---

[13] Kyle - http://oneredpaperclip.blogspot.com

opportunity to develop and demonstrate their resourcefulness. This starts well before college and we should just stop it. You may not consider yourself one of those parents ---but trust me, we have all deprived our children of demonstrating their resourcefulness--only the degree to which we have done this may vary.

Impact of Over Parenting

There are many books and studies written on the topic of child rearing in general, with guidance on how to better parent your children. There are two authors I wish to call out about how guidance directly impacts the young adult. They write about the topic of praising our young adults and the impact of how years of over parenting affects them as they transition to college.

Carol Dweck, the Lewis and Virginia Eaton Professor of Psychology at Stanford University, graduated from Barnard College in 1967 and earned a Ph.D. from Yale University in 1972. She taught at Columbia University, Harvard University, and the University of Illinois before joining the Stanford faculty in 2004. Dweck has primary research interests in motivation, personality, and development. She teaches courses in Personality and Social Development as well as Motivation. Her book, Mindset: The New Psychology of Success is a must read for all parents. Go to www.pleasedontcomehome.com for a link to her book.

For ten years Carol Dweck and her team at Columbia studied the effect of praise on students in a dozen New York schools. Her very important work included a series of experiments with 400 fifth graders.

70

The group was divided into two. Each child was given a series of puzzles that all children would be able to complete fairly well. One group of students was praised for their intelligence. They were told, "You must be smart at this." The other students were praised for their effort: "You must work really hard."

Then the students were given a choice of test for the second round. One choice was a test that would be more difficult than the first, but the researchers told the children that they'd learn a lot from attempting the puzzles. The other choice was an easy test, just like the first. Of those praised for their effort, 90 percent chose the harder set of puzzles. Of those praised for their intelligence, a majority chose the easy test. The 'smart' kids took the cop-out.

Why did this happen? The children who were praised for their intelligence learned that it was important to 'look smart, don't risk making mistakes.'

In another study Dweck demonstrated that praise could be very effective. But she cautions that all praise is not created equal. There are two key factors to effective praise. Praise must be specific and sincere. For specific suggestions of how to effectively support your student with praise, look for the section on Coaching Conversations in this chapter.

On the topic of the impact of over parenting, in her book, How to Raise an Adult: Break Free of the Overparenting Trap and Prepare Your Kid for Success, Julie Lythcott-Haims spells out the emotional impact on our young people when they are suddenly on their own. Why should we consider what Lythcott-Haims has to say? She spent years as Dean of Freshman Students at Stanford University and has witnessed new classes of brilliant yet emotionally unprepared youth. She points out that this is not unique to students at Stanford, but is widely reported among her peers at universities across the United States. In her book How to Raise an Adult, she demonstrates, through numerous studies and firsthand experience, the dire impact our over parenting is having on our children.

Many disturbing facts are shared in How to Raise an Adult. One that really jumps off the page is the 2013 American College Health Association study of close to 100,000 college students from 153 different campuses about their health. When asked about the effect of their college experiences on their health at some point over the past twelve months:

- 84.3% felt overwhelmed by all they had to do
- 79.1% felt exhausted (not from physical activity)
- 60.5% felt very sad
- 57.0% felt very lonely
- 51.3% felt overwhelming anxiety
- 46.5% felt things were hopeless
- 38.3% felt overwhelming anger
- 31.8% felt so depressed that it was difficult to function
- 8.0% seriously considered suicide
- 6.5% intentionally cut or otherwise injured themselves

She admits that there are many studies that do not prove causation of over parenting and the rise of mental health problems, but she also confirms that there are studies that do show a correlation. Depending upon the degree to which we have been over parenting, our children will guide us as to how concerned we should be about the emotional issues listed above. Every college offers resources to provide emotional support to their students. There are various names for the office providing this service, such as the Crisis Support Clinic or Counseling Services. These offices are staffed by experts in handling the challenges our students are facing and are well equipped to help them. Our role as parents is to be aware of the resources available to our students and to direct them to use these resources as appropriate.

What does it mean to be resourceful?

There are 7 key things that people who are resourceful know or do:

(1) Failing doesn't mean they are failures.
(2) Celebrate their successes – (and approximate success)
(3) Self-Advocacy
(4) FOCUS
(5) Master Meanings
(6) Stretch/Grow
(7) Be Part of a Community

1) Failing

"I've failed over and over and over again in my life and that is why I succeed." Michael Jordan

"I'm not the guy who's afraid of failure. I like to take risks, take the big shot and all that." Stephen Curry

The truth is that if you are trying new things (and you definitely should), it is likely that you will fail at some point. This is part of the natural progression of learning. Remember, failure is not a bad thing; it is a guaranteed and inevitable part of learning. In any and all new endeavors we are likely to experience some failure. Think of young toddlers learning to walk. When they fall down on the first, second or one-hundredth attempt we don't advise them to quit. Instead we encourage them to try again. This is a lesson that we forget as we get older. We try something new and when we don't achieve immediately we tend to give up or beat ourselves up.

The determining factor of successful people is that they don't sit in a corner and lick their wounds. Rather, they rebound and figure out how they can improve.

If we turn our attention to highly successful people in the area of sports, entertainment and business, each shares the same message. The difference between them and many other people is that they have developed a unique mindset: they realize that failing is an intrinsic part of succeeding. They know that every time they fail, they are learning from their mistakes. Failure is a message that tells us something could have been done differently — that there is room for improvement. And that's why successful people don't seem to care much about failing-- they never see the failure as an isolated event — but as part of a much larger process. More than that, they know that you never lose so long as you have learned something.

Imagine getting some of the feedback that these famous people have received. Our job as parents is to coach our children to recognize feedback as just that—feedback. It is not an indictment of them as people and serves to encourage them to keep moving forward.

People Who Have Failed

Albert Einstein *The German-born theoretical physicist. He developed the general theory of relativity, one of the two pillars of modern physics.*	Wasn't able to speak until almost the age of 4 and his teachers said he would 'never amount to much. [14]
Fred Astaire *An American dancer, singer, actor, choreographer, musician, and television presenter.*	A screen test report on Astaire for RKO Radio Pictures is reported to have read: "Can't sing. Can't act. Balding. Can dance a little."[15]
The Beatles *An English rock band, formed in Liverpool in 1960. They became widely regarded as the foremost and most influential act of the rock era.*	Rejected by Decca Recording Studios who said, "we don't like their sound – they have no future in show business."[16]
Steve Jobs *An American information technology entrepreneur and inventor. He was the co-founder, chairman, and chief executive officer of Apple Inc*	At 30 years old he was devastated and depressed after being removed from the company he started.[17]

[14] Einstein - http://www.theguardian.com/lifeandstyle/2005/mar/02/familyandrelationships.features11

[15] Fred Astaire - http://www.biography.com/people/fred-astaire-9190991#early-years

[16] The Beatles -The Beatles. (2000). The Beatles Anthology. San Francisco: Chronicle Books. ISBN 0-8118-2684-8

[17] Steve Jobs - Change or Die, The Second Coming of Steve Jobs by Alan Deutschman ISBN0767904338

People Who Have Failed (continued)

Oprah Winfrey *An American media proprietor, talk show host, actress, producer, and philanthropist.*	Was demoted from her job as a news anchor because she "wasn't a fit for television."[18]
JK Rowling *Author of Harry Potter series*	Lost her secretary job because she spent too much time daydreaming about a preteen wizard.[19]
Michael Jordan *An American retired professional basketball player.*	After being cut from his high school basketball team, he went home, locked himself in his room and cried.[20]
Walt Disney *An American entrepreneur, animator, voice actor, and film producer*	Was fired from a newspaper for 'lacking imagination' and 'having no original ideas.'[21]

One of the benefits of failure is that it builds resilience. The Merriam-Webster dictionary defines resilience as "the ability to become strong, healthy, or successful again after something bad happens." Let's face it, we live in

---

[18] Oprah Winfrey - 1997 Wellesley College Commencement address.
http://www.wellesley.edu/events/commencement/archives/1997commencement/commencementaddress

[19] JK Rowling - http://www.businessinsider.com/15-people-who-were-fired-before-they-became-filthy-rich-2011-4
[20] Michael Jordan - http://sports.yahoo.com/blogs/nba-ball-dont-lie/michael-jordan-really-cut-high-school-team-215707476.html
[21] Walt Disney - http://www.businessinsider.com/15-people-who-were-fired-before-they-became-filthy-rich-2011-4

challenging times and we need to prepare our children for mental toughness and resiliency. Our kids are being raised in an age of instant information, an age of harsh criticism, and an age where the world is held in constant turmoil.

In 1968, a scientist at 3M in the United States, Dr. Spencer Silver, was attempting to develop a super-strong adhesive. Instead he accidentally created a "low-tack", reusable, pressure-sensitive adhesive. For five years Dr. Silver shared his revolutionary product with colleagues at 3M, informally and in seminar presentations. An attendee at one of his seminars was Arthur Fry who worked at 3M in product development. Mr. Fry didn't immediately see the benefits. One day at church he realized that what we now know as a Post-It note would be better than the bookmark he used to mark his hymnal since it was sticky and wouldn't fall out as easily. He returned to management with his idea. It took another four years to perfect the specifications and manufacturing process[22]. In 1980 the product was introduced nationwide, fourteen years after it was created. Today this product is widely used and most of us can't imagine life without it. It was only after considerable trial and error and the tenacity of Dr. Silver and Mr. Fry that this product eventually found success. The same resilience must be applied in our own lives and those of our children.

Most everyone has had to jump some hurdles and face some failures to achieve. I have. Have you? Sometimes we forget and take for granted the successes in our lives and just how resilient we have been. Try the exercise that follows to reconnect with some of your successes and to remind yourself as you guide your student through the same process.

---

[22] http://lemelson.mit.edu/resources/art-fry-spencer-silver

Embracing Failure

It is a parent's job to teach children to embrace failure. The first thing you want them to know is that failing at something is not the same as being a failure. Our identity is the strongest thing in human nature and when we use the words 'I am' before any word we strive to align ourselves with that identity. So it is important that your children first separate their identity from the thing they attempt. The truth is that they are the opposite of a failure. Remind them that one can only fail at something if they are expanding themselves and taking on risks. Why not give them the identity of a risk taker or explorer? In fact, have them say out loud, "I am an explorer" and see how that feels.

One way to help your teens embrace failure is to share your own stories of failure. This serves several purposes:

1. They will see that like you, they can survive after a failure.
2. As a parent you are human and even you make mistakes. Many times parents operate under the illusion that they have to be perfect in the eyes of their children when really the opposite is true. Seeing that someone they hold in high regard can fail gives them confidence that if they fail, they won't lose your love and that it isn't the end of the world.

Sharing your stories can have the effect of creating a tighter bond between you and your child.

Parent Exercise: Your Failure

Think of a time that you failed at something. We all have plenty of them. On the scale of failures from 1-10 pick something no greater than a 6 or 7. Write it down. And then answer the following questions.

- *Were there lasting consequences or were you able to quickly recover and move on?*
- *What did you learn?*
- *What were you inspired to create or do as a result of this setback?*
- *What, if any, resources did you engage to correct the situation?*

The benefit of this exercise is to:

1. Remind you that failure is temporary.
2. By recalling the failure you have ready access to the memory the next time you fail. Through this memory, you will know that you can overcome future obstacles with the skills and strength you have, and your support system.
3. You now have a story ready to share with your client/student.

2) Celebrating Their Successes

When your student shares a success with you, what is your response? Do you brush over the win and push on to the next topic? Or do you perhaps give a quick 'atta boy' and then move on to the next topic?

We live in a world that is 'on' 24 hours a day and 7 days a week. It is very easy to move on to what's next and forget to stop, reflect and celebrate what's been achieved. If we ignore the wins of our students, we miss vital opportunities not only to inspire them to greater successes but also to strengthen our relationships with them. *The next section offers specific guidance on how to do this.*

Here are a couple of reasons why celebrating wins is important for you, your students and your families.

- Celebrating the wins reminds your students of the goals they set and why they set them in the first place.
- It reminds them that setting goals works! It motivates your students to continue to do great work.
- When they hit a roadblock, they have this celebration to look back on as a reminder that the current roadblock is temporary.
- Acknowledging what they did great will help them to stop and think about what they did to be successful. By shining a light on the steps to success, you help your students grasp what they perhaps had not noticed before, and tuck away the "how" for use in the future.
- It builds momentum for you and your student. Everyone is reminded that they are all capable and it puts the student one step closer to his or her overall goal.
- It moves the student's focus away from the day-to-day tasks and puts the focus, at least for a short while, on the bigger goal.
- It allows you to connect with your student in a positive way. And, some of this positivity will naturally positively affect how he/she thinks of your relationship.

In addition to celebrating your student's success, also celebrate approximate success. Remember the example provided earlier about a toddler learning to walk. When a toddler takes a step and falls, we don't admonish the child for failing to walk. We clap like crazy and get excited, which encourages the child to keep trying. Applying this to "beginner steps" with your teen may be a new concept for you. If you are reading this book you are likely to be an over achiever, especially in the ways that count the most. That's why you bought a book that offers to help you help your student achieve. A characteristic of being an achiever is having high standards. You know that when you miss your goal, rather than beating yourself up, if you acknowledge the progress that was made, it will propel you on to a course correction that will help you achieve the goal down the line.

Examples:
1. Your student has been working hard to pull his/her grades up from a low B to an A, but Instead of an A average, it's a B+. And, you clap wildly and congratulate your teen profusely because he/she is headed in the right direction. And when the excitement dies down a bit, then ask the following questions.
   - What do you think were the best improvements you made in working toward reaching your goal?
   - Is there someone you could model who has an A average?
   - Are there other resources in the form of a teacher, tutor, study group or administrator that you could engage with to think of new strategies?

2. Your student has been slow to adjust to college life, and has been complaining of being homesick. Then one day shares with you that he/she made plans to go out to the movies Friday night with a group of friends. Clap wildly and celebrate the effort it took for your

teen to get out of the comfort zone and explore something new.

3. Your student is going out for a sport/club that has a process including several elimination rounds for making the team. Each time he/she makes it through a round clap wildly. Do not clap because there is now a better chance to make the team. Clap because your student made it a step closer to her/his goal.

Clap wildly is a euphemism for however you celebrate. The point is to make it big... don't just clap but clap wildly. Let out a whistle. Stomp your feet. Do what comes naturally to you, but approach it with the same enthusiasm as you did when your child was learning to walk.

Finally, one of the most important things to remember about celebrating success is to celebrate your successes also, and to share them with your teen. By doing this you are modeling the behavior that you would like them to embrace. Additionally, by sharing your personal stories you help to move beyond the role of Supervisor and to strengthen your new relationship with your son or daughter.

3) Self-Advocacy

Claudia is a history teacher at the local community college. She had previously been teaching at the high school level and was excited to try a new challenge and to work with more mature and focused students. After all, she thought, these students are now paying money to take classes. Imagine her surprise when the first midterms approached and several of her students' parents called to advocate for their child's lack of preparation for the upcoming exam. She was shocked that at the level parents would intercede on behalf of the students.

There was one student in Claudia's class, Carol, who seemed to be more independent and successful in class as compared to her peers. Claudia decided to interview her to see if she could discern her beliefs and approach to her studies to share with her classmates. Carol shared a high school experience that taught her an important lesson about advocating for herself.

While reviewing the midterm exam one day, another student had made a compelling argument as to why the teacher should have awarded points that she took off. The teacher invited anyone in the class with the same problem to come up to her desk, and she would make an adjustment to the score. Carol decided not to bother even though she would have been due the points, as it wouldn't have raised her overall grade. A few weeks later during a parent, teacher and child conference, the teacher inquired as to why Carol didn't approach her to get the additional points. When Carol explained why, her teacher told her that she should have come up and argued her case because if she had, she would have received the few extra points on the exam, and she would have raised her midterm grade from a B to an A. The reason the teacher would have both given her the few extra exam points and raised her grade, was (1) she had been a strong performer and hard worker all year and the scoring was subjective (2) by arguing her case she would have demonstrated her commitment to success in the class and her maturity in ownership of her own success, thus showing herself deserving of being rewarded.

The moral of the story is: the squeaky wheel gets the oil—so squeak or speak up.

The four steps of self-advocacy are:
1. Understand your strengths and needs,
2. Identify your personal goals,
3. Know your legal rights and responsibilities, and
4. Communicate these to others.

How We Learn

As it relates to your student, next to understanding their strengths and needs, knowing how they best learn is important. There are three modalities (channels) by which we can learn: Visual, Auditory and/or Kinesthetic. According to the VAK or modality theory, one or two of these receiving styles is normally dominant. This dominant style defines the best way for a person to learn new information by filtering what is to be learned. This style may not always to be the same for some tasks.

| Visual | Prefer to learn through written language, such as reading and writing tasks. Visual learners remember what has been written down, even if they do not read it more than once. They like to write down directions and pay better attention to lectures if they watch them. |
| Auditory | Auditory learners often do better talking with a colleague or listening to an audio recording of the lecture or other spoken event to hear what was said. |

Kinesthetic	Kinesthetic learners do best while touching and moving. They tend to lose concentration if there is little or no external stimulation or movement. When listening to lectures they may want to take notes for the sake of moving their hands. When reading, they like to scan the material first, and then focus in on the details (get the big picture first). They typically use color highlighters and take notes by drawing pictures, diagrams, or doodling.

My daughter, Kendall, determined that she is a kinesthetic and visual learner. She has developed a note taking strategy that uses a lot of different colors and draws pictures as she takes notes in class. When she starts the school year she advises her teachers so they know that she is not goofing off but that this helps her to concentrate and learn better. Her teachers appreciate her taking ownership of her studies and communicating with them.

When she got her first job at the local smoothie shop she explained to the owner that she learned better by someone showing her what they wanted done rather than telling her. She stressed that she usually only needed to be shown once, but she knew from experience that she often missed directions when she was told what to do. By advising her new employer up front she increased the chances of her success, and diminished the possibility of his frustration had he attempted to tell her what to do, as it might have appeared that she just wasn't paying attention.

If, once your teens have identified their primary learning styles, they are challenged advocating for themselves, suggest that they describe what advice they might give a best friend who was being challenged in the classroom. Have your teens imagine that their best friend was not succeeding in class and discuss what they might suggest this friend request of the professor for support. This may sound deceivingly simple, but removing the teens one step from the situation opens up many possibilities that they may not have thought of because they were too close to it.

4) FOCUS

Focus
On One thing
Continuously
Until you achieve
Success

On May 2, 2011 Osama Bin Laden was killed by SEAL Team Six. From September 11, 2001 until that day, the United States Government had been looking for him as the leader of the Al-Qaeda group responsible for the 9-11 tragedies on American soil. In a speech by a former Navy Seal about the successful mission he shared that this team had put into practice some special strategies. First, they were maniacally focused on their target. For one year leading to the mission they did nothing that was not related to their goal. They gave up family and other outside distractions. They worked consistently as a team. They coordinated sleep, changed their diets and trained every day until Bin Laden was located. At this time they were ready to go in and complete their mission.

While your students are not faced with matters of national security, they probably have some goals that are extremely important to them. Guide them to set up a regimen to help them achieve their goals. If the goal is to get an A in the challenging organic chemistry course required for all pre-med majors, ask them to develop a list of the three things they need to do every day to reach this goal. Think of it as their Three to Thrive. We can all benefit in reaching a goal by listing our Three to Thrive— three actions, that if done consistently will have a significant positive impact on reaching our goals.

The best way to help your students with this process is to adapt it to goals of your own and then share with them what you are doing to achieve your goals. Leading by example has much more impact than telling someone what to do.

As you encourage your students to come up with their own list of things for their Three to Thrive list, you can use the following questions to prompt them.

- What is the one thing that--if you focused on it-- would allow a goal to be met?
- Is there a habit you need to eliminate or put into place?
- Is more sleep required?
- Do you need to change your diet?
- Do you need to put extra emphasis on a particular class or coursework?
- If you applied a renewed focus in this one area what is possible?

5) Master Meanings

Do you believe that two people can experience the same event and each walk away with entirely different meanings? The truth is that nothing has any meaning except the meaning we give it. Successful people know this and they master meanings by choosing a meaning for any given event throughout the day that moves them toward their goals.

Bella walked into the room of a family friend and at the same time the group burst into laughter. Naturally, as a self-conscious teenager walking into a group of teens, some of whom she knew slightly and some that she didn't know at all, she feared the worst. She assumed they were laughing at her. She left the room feeling embarrassed.

As it happens, her mom is a coaching client of mine and we had been working on mastering meanings as they related to some beliefs she had that were holding her back at work. Mom suggested to Bella that perhaps she walked into the room just as someone shared the punch line to a joke. She was encouraged to give the situation a more empowering meaning. The truth was she didn't know what had happened and it was unlikely that she would find out, so why not assign a meaning that was empowering rather than disempowering. She returned to the group of teens and ended up having a great night hanging out with what are now a new group of friends. Go Mom!

A set of twins, brother and sister, almost 30 years after it happened still assign a different meaning to something that occurred in high school. In their sophomore year the brother was sent away to boarding school. The meaning that the boy gave it was that mom and dad didn't love him very much—after all, they sent him away to go to school. The other twin, the sister, assigned the meaning that mom and dad loved him more because they invested a lot of money in his education. Who is right? We may never know. What is certain is that they both assigned disempowering meanings to the event. Think for a moment about how:

- Each of the twins felt about their relationship with their parents.
- This might have caused each twin to harbor resentment to the other.

Finding a more empowering meaning would have allowed them to more greatly enjoy what was good about the situation, experience a more joyful relationship with their parents and with one another. Instead they both carried the bitterness of what they felt was rejection for many years. This feeling of rejection colored many aspects of their lives.

I recall when one my speaking coaches gave me excellent advice about getting up in front of an audience to help with nerves. He told me, "The audience wants you to succeed." I had never thought of it that way. He proved his case by reminding me that the audience has either paid money or taken their personal time to be there, and they want their investment in money or time to be rewarded--so they really want to be satisfied. The first time I had the opportunity to speak in front of 500 people I took the stage with the confidence that 500 friends/fans were sitting in the audience. Assigning this positive element to the experience allowed me to focus on my message instead of worrying about what they might think about me. And I was rewarded by the applause of a happy audience.

If we don't master meanings they can turn into limiting beliefs. Let's say your student experiences the following: Michael walks into class and the teacher speaks gruffly to him, admonishing him to take his seat immediately. Michael might assign the meaning that the teacher doesn't like him. If this happens a couple of times then a belief is formed. The truth is that we don't know why the teacher is speaking gruffly to him. Perhaps the class before is exhausting and the teacher is anxious to get started on the next class. Perhaps Michael is consistently the last person in class and doesn't realize it. The teacher may feel that Michael's lateness everyday is holding up the class from getting started on the day's lesson. The teacher might be frustrated with Michael, but being frustrated and not liking him are not the same thing.

Common limiting beliefs of students
- My teacher doesn't like me.
- I can't figure this out.
- I don't have the tools I need.
- This is too hard. I am not smart enough.
- I don't have the money I need.
- Nobody likes me.

To demolish a limiting belief you need only to imagine if the opposite were true and think about how you would behave. Use the examples below to guide your sons and daughters to try on the appropriate new belief and then ask the questions that follow. What I mean by try on the new belief is to have them say it out loud a few times with enthusiasm. To have the desired impact they need to say it like they mean it. Acknowledge that this might feel silly and awkward at first but ask them to play along. Point out their current belief isn't working so there is no harm in trying something new.

Limiting belief = My teacher doesn't like me.
Try instead ➔ My teacher loves me!

Follow up questions to ask your son or daughter:
- With this belief what would you do differently?
- What would you ask of the teacher?
- How might you act in class?
- Would you raise your hand more?
- Might you go to the teacher with ideas and/or questions?
- How would you feel about completing assignments?
- How would you walk into class?

Limiting belief = This is too hard. I am not smart enough.
Try instead ➔ I might not know how to do this now, but I am smart and I can figure it out!

Follow up questions to ask your son or daughter:
- With this belief what resources would you call on to help you learn?
- Would you spend more time or less time learning the concepts?

Limiting belief = Nobody likes me here.
Try instead ➔ Everybody loves me here. They are just waiting for me to arrive.

Follow up questions to ask your son or daughter:
If you believed this would you:
- Smile more?
- Go out to more events with others?
- Volunteer to help someone who looks like he/she might not fit in?
- Introduce yourself first in a new setting?

Once your sons and daughters have answers to the questions that apply to their situations, challenge them to behave just that way for the next three weeks and see what changes they notice. At first some of these exercises might be a little uncomfortable as they try on a new behavior. If they are nervous about trying this, have them think about a person they know who exhibits the new belief and then pretend to be that person.

Sophia was uncomfortable about meeting new people. Her best friend, Kathy, always seemed to meet new people with ease. She decided that when she goes to college she is going to pretend she is Kathy for the first month. She will say the things Kathy would say, dress the way she dresses, act the way Kathy acts. This is not to suggest that Kathy is better than she is. However, in this one area, Kathy has achieved a level of success that Sophia would like to achieve.

Carla and Barbara met in a one-week intensive class and partnered to work on assignments as was required by the teacher. Carla was very outgoing and Barbara a bit shy. As far as their ability to understand and apply the class concepts, they were equally matched. However, Barbara never raised her hand to answer a question posed by the teacher and Carla frequently did. The very wise teacher noticed what was happening and took Barbara aside to find out what was preventing her from participating since participation would be part of the final grade. He challenged her to model Carla's behavior the next class. He suggested that she sit the same way, breathe the same way and speak up in the same way. Carla agreed to do this. The next day she came in and sat the way Carla did and raised her hand with conviction. She easily answered the questions posed to her. Everyone in the class noticed the difference right away and it opened the door for her to make new friends. Prior to the experiment, she had been reluctant to meet her other classmates. The teacher and her classmates positively rewarded the new behavior and over time she started answering questions without needing to model her partner, Carla.

6) Stretch/Grow

"If you want something you've never had, you must be willing to do something you've never done." Thomas Jefferson

Leo Burnett was an American advertising executive and the founder of the Leo Burnett Company, Inc. He was responsible for creating some of advertising's most well-known 20th century characters and campaigns including Tony the Tiger, Charlie the Tuna, the Marlboro Man, the Maytag Repairman, United Airline's "Fly the Friendly Skies," Allstate's "Good Hands."[23] His guiding philosophy was "when you reach for the stars you may not quite get one, but you won't come up with a handful of mud either." [24] This was used as a reminder to his team to strive for greatness in all of their work.

There are many benefits to stretching and growing, particularly for young people. For most of us, our late teens and early 20's are a great time for exploration. Through exploration we learn more about what we like and don't like. New experiences, especially in an area in which a person is interested can help to either confirm these interests or encourage a change of course.

At my children's high school there are two classes designed for the students to deep dive into their areas of interest. As juniors they have a class in which they do an independent study in their chosen area of interest. My daughter, Hattie, is interested in politics. Her junior year coincided with a gubernatorial election year so she decided to focus her independent study on how the gubernatorial candidates

---

[23] Burnett campaigns "CNBC Titans: Leo Burnett". Hulu. CNBC.

[24] Stars – www.leoburnett.com

communicated their messages to the public. I recall driving her to several debates, and we have photos of her with each of the Republican and Democratic candidates. These hands-on experiences allowed her to take what she had learned in the classroom and see how valid the conclusions she had drawn were.

Ultimately, she was selected to present her findings to a countywide audience. Then, as a senior, she was able to secure an internship with a local judge, with the assistance of mentors. Each Friday she attended court with the judge. On Wednesdays she worked in chambers with the judge. Her focus was on youth in the judicial system. She took several field trips to other courts throughout the year. By the end of the year she had a very good understanding of the court system that was instrumental in helping to confirm for her that she would like to pursue a legal career.

At the end of each year the students from both classes get together in the school library, science fair style, with poster presentations displaying the findings of the juniors and PowerPoint presentations by the seniors. Both years, as I toured the many presentations, I was so impressed with what the teens had learned and were able to share with the parents and visitors in the room. At the conclusion of one presentation I asked the young woman if she thought she might pursue this area as a career. Her reply was 'absolutely not'. What a wonderful response. So much better to learn after a small investment of 9 months that this was not something she wanted to do, instead of dedicating years of education only to discover later that this was not what she wanted after all.

To follow are ideas for how students can stretch and grow.

Travel

There's a whole big world out there. By broadening their perspectives our young adults can experience other ways of thinking. This point isn't made to imply that some other person's way of thinking is better than our own. Rather, every time we hear another perspective we can try it, own it for a while to see how it fits. We can keep parts that make sense to us and let go of those that do not.

Recently, I ran into a young man who had taken the opportunity to do a summer exchange program to Spain. He excitedly recounted his experience for me, highlighting how much fun he had experienced and the people he met and what he had learned about himself and the country. You should know that 6 months had passed by the time we had the conversation and his level of enthusiasm was still extremely high. You may be thinking I can't afford to send my teenager to Europe for the summer. There are many affordable options through the schools for your student to have this experience. The young man who shared his experience with me is the son of 1ˢᵗ generation immigrants with more meager means than many in this country. What they have in common with all other parents is, they want the best for their child and figured out a way to successfully pursue this experience.

Once students get to college there are often scholarships available to them to make this type of exchange possible. The best resource for this is to have your student check with the college office that handles study abroad. Typically, the school will have an office with either the words 'Study Abroad', 'Global Experience' or 'Global Education' included in the title. If not, check with the Student Affairs Office, they should be able to point you in the right direction. There are many options offered to students with varying times away. There are programs for a full year, a semester, a summer or even over a school break. There are programs to meet your student explorer's area of interest and your wallet.

Visit a Friend's Family

Some of my fondest memories in college were the times I spent with my roommate's family. They were somehow the same as my family, and different all at the same time. Everything from how they set the table, celebrated holidays and their dinner discussions was different than the same activity with my own family. What I learned in the process was that there was a whole different way of doing things than in my narrow view of the world.

I met my roommate's relatives and learned about different careers and ways of living. I will never forget her grandfather. Each winter he would spend 6 weeks living in another country. It was the first time I had heard the expression, "he winters in Aruba." Fortunately, my roommate and I were welcomed each year to stay with him for our-week of spring break. I decided right then that I wanted to emulate his lifestyle. It may sound silly and not like a really important goal, but I was taking a stand for how I wanted to live life one day and it was independent from how my own parents and grandparents lived. What is important about the lesson this delivers is the independent thinking and seeing myself in a life of my choosing, not my parents' life or anyone else's for that matter.

7) Become Part of a Community

Depending on your student's sense of self, the transition to college can be super easy or a bit of a challenge. Encourage her/him to get involved from week 1. There are many ways and activities through which he/she will meet other students with something in common. This includes a broad array of clubs that cover the full interest spectrum, through which they will develop friends and a sense of belonging.

Why join a club? The truth is that even the most confident of teens can feel a little lost as they establish themselves in a new environment. Remind your teen that many people feel a little lost and that everyone will need to make some adjustments to their new environment. Some students may come to college with a friend but most do not. If they are part of something, they won't feel so alone. And joining a club will introduce them to others who have similar interests.

The other benefit to joining a club is to give students the satisfaction of helping their peers. Depending on the club, your son or daughter may find a role model who will help her/him maneuver the hills and valleys of college life. Or, in time, your student may find fulfillment serving as a role model to another student. While the degree may vary, we all have a need to contribute. A great way to do this is to challenge your teen to think about how some other person might be struggling to fit in. This challenge accomplishes two goals. First, it meets the need to contribute and it also changes the focus from a student's own struggle to something else. Your student will quickly learn that the easy way to help someone is by taking the lead, saying hello and introducing himself/herself to someone. This is a great way to contribute to a person's comfort in a new environment.

You may be thinking –BUT--they are there for an education and schoolwork must come first. Yes you are correct, but their emotional well being and feeling of belonging will have a tremendous impact on their success in all aspects of their time at school.

Tip! : If your students are particularly reluctant to "get involved," you might share a situation of your own in which you felt uncomfortable and how you overcame it. You can suggest making a game out of it. Ask them to report back to you on how many new people they met in one day.

What's Next? The Next Phase?

At this time, parents can best help their student by transitioning from the role of Supervisor to Trusted Advisor. For the first 18 years of our lives as parents, it is our job to supervise most aspects of our children's lives. We supervise what food they eat, what activities they join, their chores, and as they get older their comings and goings.

Coaching Conversations

As part of your new role as Trusted Advisor you will also assume the role of coach. To follow are some examples of coaching conversations, some do's and don'ts and the really hard stuff for parents to master.

A coach's job is to help their client (student) to:
- get unstuck
- create healthy habits
- have more fun

- unleash creativity
- improve relationships
- develop leadership potential
- identify and reach goals

What follows are some examples of coaching conversations to support you in potential conversations that you may find yourself having with your son or daughter.

Scenario 1

Your son calls you on the phone to share that he got an A on an exam after struggling in a class.

Good Response
Great job!

Better Response
Great job son! I am really proud of you. What do you think was the key to you getting an A?

Best Response
Great job son! Are you proud of yourself? What do you think was the key to you getting an A? Is there anything you would do differently to make it even easier to get the A next time? I am really proud of your commitment to your goals. You are on the right track! Thanks for sharing your success with me. How else will you celebrate your success?

One of the things that we don't learn in school is how to give a compliment or to support someone. As was previously addressed in the discussion about Carol Dweck (p.70), praise must be specific and sincere. A cursory 'great job' runs the risk of seeming insincere to the person receiving the compliment. By being specific about what you are proud of, it's clear to the recipient that you are paying attention and are fully involved in the conversation. This shows your student that you give his/her achievement a very high level of importance. We live in a time when people are more focused on their 'me machine' (also known as their smart phone) than on what is happening around them. Being specific in what you say demonstrates that you are giving the person you are addressing what people often crave most, your attention. In the above scenario, what's very important is showing that you are proud of the student's commitment to his goals.

Scenario 2

Your student calls to lament about not making it on to the team of his/her desire.

Good response
I feel so sorry for you. I can't believe you didn't make the team. What were they thinking?

Better response
I know you must feel so frustrated right now. I am sorry you are feeling this way. Why do you think you didn't make the team?

Best response
I know you must feel so frustrated right now. I am sorry you are feeling this way. What can you learn from this to take forward? I am proud of you right now. You could have buried your head in frustration or even embarrassment. But, by sharing how you feel and learning from it, you have an opportunity to grow. I'm going to celebrate your learning

something new…and you should too! How will you celebrate?

Scenario 3

Your student is beating her/himself up for not meeting an academic goal.

Good response
I see you are really frustrated about not getting an A after you worked so hard.

Better response
I see you are really frustrated. I also notice that you went from a D on your last test to a B on this one. That's outstanding! You raised it 2 full letter grades in one step!

Best response
I see you are really frustrated. I also notice that you went from a D on your last test to a B on this one. That's outstanding! You raised it 2 full letter grades in one step! Do you think you are a success? If not, what has to happen in order for you to feel successful?

If the student replies that only meeting the goal will allow her/him to feel successful, then let's check in on their rules for feeling success. Remind her/him that if a batter in professional baseball can get a hit in three out of ten at bats, giving him a batting average of .300, he is considered a very good hitter. In Major League Baseball, no batter has had better than a .400 average

Scenario 4

Your student is attending a university with very selective admissions criteria and is feeling frustrated because he/she is accustomed to being at the top of the class and is now one among many students who excel.

Good response
You are still the amazing student I know and love.

Better response
You worked hard to earn a spot among a group of gifted and focused learners. That's an incredible achievement. So many people have felt despair when they didn't get accepted to your school and you earned a spot. Hold your head high because you are still the amazing student I know and love.

Best response
Wow! What a great opportunity to take your game to a higher level. You have an excellent foundation upon which to build. You are still the amazing student I know and love. What an incredible opportunity to surround yourself with other gifted and focused students. Imagine what you can create/achieve together. Who are the 2 or 3 people you want to collaborate with first?

Your Job Is To Help With The W's And L's

Your student will surely face some obstacles in college. It's part of the growth process. In every competition there are W's and L's. And no, it's not that there are Winners and Losers but preferably, there are Winners and Learners. What makes us successful is using learning to help us be better prepared next time. It's our job as parent/Trusted Advisor to help shift the focus to the learning.

For most of us, the conversations above represent new concepts, a new role and new ways recommended to coach our children. And like anything else, it will take some practice to become adept at the skill. Now that you are seeing a new approach, continue to look for opportunities to hone these new skills.

Do's and Don'ts

As you develop these new skills, keep in mind, there are some basic Do's and Don'ts to help guide you:

Do's

Keep the lines of communication open and express your commitment to moving to a new relationship with your emerging young adults as they move from being dependent to becoming independent. Your new role as Trusted Advisor is to support them without solving their problems for them.

Don'ts

1 – Don't visit campus more than one time a semester unless you are going to support an event. You've been to college; this is your child's time. One of the reasons we send them to college is for them to gain some independence…and it's time for you to get a life! Learn more about getting on with your life in the bonus chapter at the end of this book.

2 – Don't pick their courses. It's incumbent upon your students to understand graduation requirements and to select courses that will help them reach their goal. Part of growing to independence is understanding you don't have to make every decision on your own. There are people with expertise in different areas. Now is the time for your student to start developing a network of experts upon whom to call. Most colleges have counselors/advisors to assist in course selection to ensure the student is on the right track to complete his/her chosen program and its requirements.

3 – Don't communicate with your student's professors. By communicating with his/her professors you are undermining your student--you are basically saying that you don't think he/she is competent to manage his/her own affairs. It also raises doubts in the mind of the professor about the student. The professor will wonder what is wrong with this student, why does he/she need mommy or daddy to communicate with me? Are mommy and daddy doing the student's class work as well? And finally, it isn't the job of the professor to communicate with you. Professors have enough on their plates without this extra responsibility.

4 – Don't solve their problems.
That your student reaches out to you with small problems is a behavior we've conditioned our children to do while they were growing up. I know that I have been guilty of this very thing. Once my children had cell phones it became so easy for them to text from school with a quick "I forgot my lunch" or "I left my important school paper on the kitchen counter." My justification for swooping in to save the day was that I worked from home and it was simple to take a little break to run up to school to drop off the forgotten item. The truth was, they would survive if they missed lunch one day and truthfully, they could find another way to eat. As

far as the forgotten homework assignment, turning it in was just as important as completing it. By solving these problems for my kids, I deprived them of the opportunity to learn from their mistakes and to understand every action has a consequence.

As parents, we have to learn that when our children text from college with a problem, we must resist the temptation to solve it immediately. Wait a couple of hours or days to give them the opportunity to solve it on their own. This will empower them to be more resourceful and less dependent.

So what happens when there is a bigger problem like their cable TV or electricity was turned off? This is a great opportunity to learn about consequences. They will have to be resourceful and figure out who else can help them. How do they get the electricity turned back on? Do they need a ride to the electric company office to pay the bill in person? Do they need to stay with a friend who has electricity for a couple of days? Sometimes the best memories are created from adversity.

Parent Exercise:

Write down the three biggest challenges (problems) you had when you were in college.

How did you solve each problem?

What, if any, role did your parents play in solving the problems?

What were the gifts in the problems?

The point of this exercise is to remind you of the many challenges you resolved without your parents fixing things for you. They knew that you were naturally creative, resourceful and whole and as such you would find your own resolution. Another way of saying this is, they trusted you to find your way. It is time for us to remember that our children are equally as creative and resourceful.

Chief Talk: If I weren't here to solve this problem how would you handle it?

The direction given in this chapter is tough. It's tough for parents not for our children. The problem with our children is <u>us</u>. Let's just acknowledge that now. It's time to break the pattern of managing our "kids" as we've done for 18 years. This direction more than that in other chapters will require us to stand back and observe some train wrecks. You will have to be ready to tolerate some anxiety, self-doubt and failure in your children and in yourself as parent.

6

Investment

"A budget is telling your money where to go instead of wondering where it went."

Dave Ramsey
American Financial Author

Investment is defined as the action or process of investing money for profit or material result. To really master investment you need to have more than basic financial skills. What your student will need is to get on a path to money mastery so as to start life after college debt-free.

Money mastery means that you understand the long-term impact of your financial decisions, and that every time you earn or spend money you are making a decision that will impact your future. I am reminded of the story about the UPS employee. In October of 1991 The New York Times reported, "Theodore R. Johnson never made more than $14,000 a year, but he invested wisely -- so wisely that he made $70 million. Now he is donating $36 million of his fortune for education."

One of the key elements of money mastery is living debt-free. The cost of education in the United States today is so exorbitantly expensive that only a small percentage of

110

students will leave college with no debt. That said, we need to think carefully about how much debt you and your student want to take on and how you can limit this debt by attending a great local state school to eliminate room and board expense or by winning scholarships.

What **is** avoidable is credit card debt. When students head off to college they are offered credit cards, and many fall into the trap of I want rather than I need. What they don't consider is how quickly the interest accrues and how long it will take to get out of debt.

Why is it important to not only ensure that your students hone their financial skills but also achieve a mastery of money? There are many reasons, including:
- it's better to end life with more money than you need;
- the impact in forty years on someone who starts life after college with debt and one who doesn't is dramatically different;
- starting to consistently save early is important; and
- people who are not worried about how to pay their basic living expenses experience less stress.

One day my sixteen year old said to me, "Mom, why doesn't granddaddy work?" I thought for a minute and realized that for all of her life he hadn't worked. He retired early at age fifty-eight and hasn't worked for the last eighteen years. I wouldn't define him as wealthy but he has more than enough money for some travel and to pursue his hobbies of tennis and golf. He regularly pursues his passions and owns two homes; one of which is in a vacation spot. He had a successful career, but what really allows him to live so comfortably is that he was very thoughtful about how he spent his money. He was always a saver and was able to send all three of his children to private colleges. His financial acumen is something that we should model.

| Chief Talk: Spend less than you earn. |

One of the companions of poor planning is the stress related to poor financial management. The most obvious impact of stress is the toll it takes on your health. In fact, research suggests that stress also can bring on or worsen certain symptoms or diseases.

Parent Exercise:

Before you can advise your student on money mastery, take a moment and consider the impact that money has in your life. As you do this exercise keep in mind that we all can benefit from improving our own money mastery. The purpose of this exercise is to understand how our decisions about money impact our choices and freedom.

Reminder: doing these exercises will put you in a better position to advise your student.

1 - Write down your monthly expenses. This may include:
- *Mortgage*
- *Car note 1*
- *Car note 2*
- *Electric, gas, water or other utility bill*
- *Cable/Phone bill*
- *Health Insurance*
- *Credit Card Debt*
- *Other expenses: Food, gas, misc*

2 – Total the monthly expenses

3 – If you were not obligated to pay these bills would you:
- *Spend your time and energy differently?*
- *Would you have the same job?*
- *Who would you fire from your life? What is meant by this is that who are we keeping in our life just to split the bills or who contributes in some other way to our monthly bills.*

As you complete this exercise are there lessons that you can take forward to share with your student? One of the lessons might be that throughout our lives we should strive to continue to learn more and improve our choices. This knowledge will also provide you with some real life examples, as appropriate, to share with your young adult. Real life examples are important, as people tend to learn and remember more when the lesson is shared via a story.

The Sure-Fire Way to Reduce Stress

The most effective driver of financial health is having a budget—and adhering to it. Similar to our discussion in chapter 4, a budget is like having a financial vision and a roadmap all in one. One of my clients once told me that he didn't want to have a budget because he wanted to be free to buy what he wanted when he wanted. He didn't want someone telling him that he shouldn't spend $6 at Starbucks every day. I agreed with him. If he wants to spend $6 at Starbucks every day then he should. He just needs to add it to his budget. The challenge with not budgeting, but spending $6 a day at Starbucks, is that he may be risking his ability to make another more important purchase or payment. By defining goals and, creating a vision for his finances and a roadmap for how to get there, he will dramatically increase his ability to meet his financial goals and reduce the stress in his life.

Simply put, creating a budget decreases your stress level because, with a budget, there are no surprises. What we <u>can</u> count on are unexpected problems or opportunities. Car problems or unexpected medical bills have a way of showing up at the worst time. What if your friends called one day to offer you the opportunity join them on a dream vacation. The cost of housing is paid for, you just need to buy your airline ticket. With a budget in place, you don't have to panic or wonder if you have the money—you already know. This sense of financial clarity is important not only in college, but throughout life.

Let's Talk About Money

The first thing you will want to do to is address the importance of having a budget to open the dialogue about money. Don't assume it is being discussed or taught at school. It isn't. If you have been covering most of your children's expenses, they may not have ever really thought much about money. That said, they probably do have some beliefs about money…your beliefs.

Parent Exercise:
Complete the sentence:
Money is_____.

This simple exercise can reveal some of the
limiting beliefs about money that you have
unwittingly passed along to your children.

Top Limiting Beliefs About Money

Limiting Belief	What It's Communicating	Empowering Belief
Money is the root of all evil.	This is a common misconception if you haven't mastered this area of your life yet. Or perhaps you had a bad experience with rich people.	Money is neutral and a resource to do good in my life.
Money isn't that important. It's only money.	Not taking money seriously is probably why you haven't achieved a more satisfying relationship with money.	Money is one of my priorities in life.

Top Limiting Beliefs About Money (cot'd)

The rich get richer and the poor get poorer.	This is just an excuse. It allows you to give up any power that you have to impact your financial situation.	My financial situation is primarily up to me.
I'm not good with money.	[Yet.] This belief has an underlying assumption that you can't learn new things…is this true? Of course not.	I continuously learn more and use my knowledge about money.
My family has never been rich.	If you live in the United States you have no limitations and the past does not equal the future.	I can create my financial independence by learning and acting on what I learn.

This list represents just a few of the most common limiting beliefs about money. If any of the limiting beliefs have been yours in the past you will want to start to change your language and thinking about them. Try using the language in the far right column to start changing your thinking about these beliefs.

It is crucial that you talk with and warn your student about credit—and emphasize the necessity not to open a credit card without discussing it with you. It is common early in the new school year for credit card companies to visit campuses, post signs encouraging college freshman to sign up for a credit card. Without a cautionary discussion your student may just sign up for a credit card or two the first week on campus when he/she sees friends signing up.

Chief Talk: Save your money, you will come to a want.

Help Your Student Develop a Budget

Help your student address these five essential steps to budgeting:

(1) What are my financial goals?
(2) Where does my money come from? (Income)
(3) What do I spend money on? (Expenses)
(4) Pull it all together (Surplus or Deficit)
(5) Time to adjust (if necessary)

Since this is likely quite new, and perhaps a somewhat daunting step for your student, you will want to sit and work through these steps with her/him.

Step 1: What are my financial goals?

*Be sure your student understands that this is the **most** important step in the process.*

Many people skip over this step or do not give it adequate attention. As a young adult, your student's ability to succeed or fail in reaching his/her budgeting goals is decided in this step. The purpose of a budget is not only to stay out of debt, but also to maximize enjoyment. Thus, the first step in creating a budget is to set financial goals.

Some possible goals for your student to consider include:
- Minimize the debt I graduate with
- Spring break travel
- Save for a car
- A graduation trip through Europe
- A down payment for a home

Help your student as he/she works through the following: Be sure to select something that inspires you. Select something that creates a compelling future for you. There is not one answer that fits everyone. You may have to make some tough choices but with the completion of this step of the budgeting process, it will make any sacrifices less painful because you will be focused on what you are getting and not what you are giving up.

Remember that in chapter 4 we talked about SMART goals: Specific, Measurable, Attainable, Relevant and Time Specific. You will want to follow the same rules for developing a goal for your budget. Let's use these 3 categories for your goals:

Short Term – less than one year

Mid Range – one to three years
Long Term – more than five years

Ask your student to use this as an example:
Let's say you are planning on a two month backpacking trip through Europe to celebrate when you graduate. Let's assume you set this goal at the end of freshman year so you have 36 months to plan. After a bit of research you discover that with some economizing you can take your trip for $3600. This means you will need to save $100/month.

Great! You have just helped your student set her/his first SMART budget goal.

S – Specific – You plan to travel through Europe for 6 weeks

M – Measurable – You know you will need $3600

A – Attainable – You will need to save $100/month

R – Relevant – Your desire to travel through Europe makes it relevant to you as a reward for your hard work.

T – Time specific – you plan to reach your goal in 3 years

Some other examples of goals your student might set before heading off to college include:
- Travel on spring break with friends
- Buy a car when you graduate
- Down payment for a home when you graduate
- Save for graduate school

Go to www.pleasedontcomehome.com to get your financial goals forms.

Step 2: Where does my money come from?

Have your student list all of her/his sources of income, (work, student loans, family, social media, online business) and the amount that comes from each source each month.

If he/she gets one disbursement per semester (e.g. scholarships or student loans), you will want to advise the student: take out your non-recurring costs like tuition and books and then divide what remains by the number of months in the semester.

Student Example: If you earn $300/month and you have $1,200 left over from student loans after you pay your non-recurring semester fees and there are 4 months in the semester, then your total monthly income is $600. ($1,200/4=$300 + $300)

Continue to assist your student as he/she works through each step. Offer to help address each question and exercise as needed.

Step 3: What do I spend money on?

Have you ever had that horrible feeling at the end of the month trying to figure out "where did all of my money go?" Before you can manage your money you need to know what you are spending it on. For one month keep track of every expense you have. This is probably most easily done on your phone. There are many apps that can help you do it. Or, you may find it easier to review your expenses in a spreadsheet.

Next you will want to separate your expenses into three categories:

Fixed – Necessary expenses that stay the same from month to month, e.g. rent (apartment or dorm), if dorm, food may be a fixed cost
Variable – Necessary expenses that vary from month to month, e.g. food, gas
Wants – Discretionary expenses, e.g. movies, eating out, clothing

You may not see the value in categorizing your expenses now, but you will when we get to step 5. Your tuition and books are not included in this budget. Only recurring expenses are included.

Tip! Include your monthly savings goal as part of your list of expenses. You will have much greater success in reaching your goal if it is part of your budget. This may be a challenge but even if you have to start small ($5) include an amount to save in your budget. Saving and paying yourself first should be a lifelong habit. College is a great time to start this habit.

Step 4: Pull it all together (Surplus or Deficit)

When you take your income and subtract your expenses what remains? If it is a positive number we call it a monthly surplus and if it is a negative number you have a deficit. So long as it isn't zero you now have a decision to make. With a surplus you can start saving towards another goal, put more money toward your primary goal or invest it. If you have a deficit go on to step 5.

Step 5: Time to adjust (if necessary)

This is where the categorizing of expenses you did in step 3 will come in handy.

Begin with your 'Wants'. Do you need to cut back on the number of lattes, meals out or movies you allow for each month? If you reduce the amount you budgeted for this each month will that help you to balance your budget?

If the answer is no you will need to review your Variable expenses in the short term. Do you need to be more mindful about turning all of the lights off when you leave your apartment? Is it more cost effective to take the bus rather than drive your car and pay parking fees?

Finally, if you are still unable to balance your budget you will need to review your fixed expenses and make an adjustment. This will be more difficult to do because it may represent a necessity such as the apartment lease you signed. This may be your indication to find a cheaper housing solution next year.

On the website, www.pleasedontcomehome.com, there are some links to websites with ideas for saving money. There are also some files and spreadsheets to get you started on your budget.

7

Transformation

"Take advantage of every opportunity to practice your communication skills so that when important occasions arise, you will have the gift, the style, the sharpness, the clarity, and the emotions to affect other people."

Jim Rohn, an American entrepreneur, author and motivational speaker

A transformation is defined as a complete or major change. Transforming from an insecure college freshman to a successful and confident young adult comes down to communication. The ability to convey thoughts clearly and effectively is the key to independence.

This chapter is divided into two sections. Section one describes the importance of the ability of your student--now a young adult—to communicate with you, his/her parents as an independent adult. As your student transitions to young adult, it is important that you reach a level of comfort communicating with her/him as two adults, rather than parent and child. The second section in this chapter stresses the importance of every adult being able to effectively communicate with others.

Communication Plan (on the path to independence from parents)

One of the first things we, as parents, need to do is set some expectations for how we will communicate with our college students as they progress in their self-awareness and begin moving toward independence. It is important for us to recognize that it isn't about us. The time has come for us to let go. This is much more difficult for the parent than for most young adults. And once communication expectations are set, it will be helpful to structure a plan.

In setting communication expectations it is essential to define those topics that are off limits and those that are in limits.

In Limits/Off Limits

First, it's important to let your young adults know that they are still in your heart even if they no longer are living in your home. Over the four years they are away at school the topics that you discuss with them will change. They will mature over time, and each subsequent year of college they will acclimate more to campus life and begin preparing for life after college.

Some examples of what you will want to know about your young adults' freshman year:
  • Assure them that you want to know about their social lives.
  • What clubs have they joined?
  • What friends have they made?

- Be sure to inquire about how their classes are coming along.

Things that are off limits include solving basic problems such as if they neglected to pay the electric bill and now the electricity has been cut off.

What you want to do is encourage independence. You can do this by giving them the opportunity to problem solve, make new friends and develop new resources.

Why do you need to have a communication plan?
It's important to lay the groundwork for communication. Depending on your young adult, you may need to establish the importance of any and all communication. It's okay to admit to them that you will miss them. Of course, neither of you may feel that way 6 months leading up to their departure. Young adults will generally be trying to exert their independence—and parents generally try to hold on to what little control they still have. It can be a trying time eventually leading you to think a little distance could be a good thing. That feeling will pass quickly.

Cell phones are a game changer. We live in an age in which an immediate response is expected. And we have been conditioned over the years to respond to our children's wants and needs quickly. Now that they are in college and not around the corner the request becomes: Can you send me …? And the "can you send me" has a much higher price tag. Alternatively, you should encourage independence. You can do this by giving them the opportunity to problem solve, make new friends and develop new resources.

The Goldilocks Phenomenon

Just like Goldilocks, we are looking for the solution that is 'just right.' To achieve this, you will want to work to strike a balance in the frequency and topics on which you communicate.

The Water Bottle

Right before my daughter, Hattie, left for college I encouraged her to spend a little extra money on a nice water bottle, thinking that if she liked the bottle she might drink more water. About two weeks after I dropped her off at school I got a phone call. "Mom, you are going to be so disappointed in me." I couldn't imagine what she was talking about. "Mom, I lost my water bottle." I remained silent and she went on about where she thought she might have left it and that she would be more responsible going forward and that she had already ordered a new one. I smiled to myself as I was pleased that she wasn't asking me to solve the problem for her but a little troubled that she felt she had to confess to me. I reminded Hattie that I love her dearly and that I am always here to support her. I am here to counsel her, celebrate with her and to listen to her when she is faced with a challenge. At the same time she needn't feel that she must report every little incident to me.

One of our other tasks as parents is to alleviate our children's guilt for not communicating, whatever their age. As parents we have to remember it isn't about us. The reason it's important for our teens to communicate with us is not just because we miss them, but also so that we know they are doing well at school. Doing well "at school" doesn't just mean that they are achieving good grades, but equally important, that they are doing well emotionally.

Every student is different in terms of how they adjust when they are away at school. But for every student it is an adjustment—for some, more difficult than for others. It's a new environment and for many it may be the first time they have shared a living space with a non-family member. If they are doing well we can limit our communication. In fact we will want to temper any guilt they might have for not being better at communication. It may seem like the point being made conflicts with the point that was just made. It is best to explain through a story.

Typically Hattie and I have a quick chat each week. Every couple of days we usually send a text sharing a joke or picture. Sometimes, because my work often requires me to travel, I have limited availability to talk for up to two weeks. After not talking to my daughter for 2 weeks, I texted her on a Saturday morning to see if she might have time to talk with her mom. She called about 20 minutes later and we started what would be a 2-hour chat. (I remember when I was in college and could never have a lengthy chat with my mother due to the cost.) She shared many funny stories about going out with her girlfriends, about her classes and generally about how much fun she was having at school. After a while, and completely to my surprise, she burst into tears. When I inquired as to the problem. She said, "Mom, sometimes I don't miss you at all and I feel guilty." I almost burst out laughing. I was so happy that she felt guilty about it. She went on to say that nighttime was the toughest time for her because she missed our nighttime rituals we practiced when she lived at home.

I assured her that I missed her every day and people often asked me how I was adjusting to her absence. The thing that made this less painful was knowing that she was happy and engaged in her new life.

Some of the best ways to keep in touch are:

Communication Method	Benefits
E-Mail	This is a great way to share information that is not urgent. And a great way to prepare your teens for the future. Many young people do not seem to like using email as a means of regular communication. However, many companies prefer this as a primary form of communication, as it creates a written record of what was "said.".
Snail Mail	There is nothing like getting an actual piece of mail. Even the most jaded of teens will have smiles on their faces when they get a picture of the family dog or a word of encouragement in something they can hold in their hands. Of course, if there is a $20 bill that has been slipped in too, it's even more appreciated.

Some of the best ways to keep in touch (continued):

Talk on the phone	There really is no substitute for hearing your child's voice or them yours.
Text	This is most likely your student's favorite form of communication. It's great for a quick check in, but not appropriate for any meaningful exchange. Texting can also be a great form of one-way communication. It's a great way to remind your child to call grandma for her birthday. It's also great for sending a word of encouragement.
Facebook (or other social media)	If you are fortunate enough to be 'friends' with your student on social media, remember it's a privilege and not a right. Don't abuse it with comments on every picture or post. If you are constantly commenting or liking posts your student will feel like he/she is being watched and that may be a big turnoff.

Care Packages	This is one of those things that has been around since the first students went off to college and is still appreciated by every teen (or young adult). There are companies out there now who will create themed (think mid terms or holidays) ones or you can make your own. I know one group of ladies who get together regularly to make and send packages to their children away at college. You can even get creative! One parent I know sent her teen fall leaves from the tree outside their home because she attended school in a warm climate.
Skype/FaceTime	This is the best invention ever for a college student living away from home. Be sure to schedule regular times where you get to see their (and they get to see your) face.

Social Media

As a Trusted Advisor it is important to follow your student on social media and the web. Often times as students exert their independence at college they may be captured in less than ideal or even compromising photos. These pictures may seem like fun, but they can have big repercussions. Employers will review any and all public information available to them to make a hiring decision. This only makes sense because once you are hired you become a brand ambassador. One might argue that what I do on my personal time is my own business and that is an accurate statement. But, understand that there is a great likelihood that there will be consequences. On social media we are building an image and identity for ourselves, which in a sense is our individual brand. If your students challenge this thought ask them what image a person seeking admittance to a top law school (substitute their goal) might want her/his brand image to be. And then suggest that they confirm that their social brand matches this.

Setting Up A Communication Plan

The first thing you have to do is consider your son or daughter. What follows is not 'one size fits all' advice. Generally speaking, boys are different from girls. And, this (in part) will drive how much they need and want to communicate with parents. Also, moms and dads may communicate differently with their teens. You will also want to consider how communicative your teens have been during their high school years. If for the last year all you have received has been grunts as they passed you in the hall, there is no reason to expect that things will suddenly be different now that they are at college.

With these considerations in mind, it is important to establish a plan for communicating before they head off to college. Establish now how frequently you will communicate. Determine if communicating with one parent will be sufficient or will each parent need/want communication? What will you want to know about? What will you communicate to them?

Schedule

Schedule your calls or FaceTime using whatever works best for your family. Perhaps it's every (or every other) Sunday afternoon or evening as you both get prepared for the week. But it's important that you both know you will have that chance to talk and catch up.

What do you talk about? For some readers this section might seem silly as you have an ongoing dialogue with your children and you have a very communicative teen. If that's true feel free to skip this. Keeping in mind that the purpose of this call is mostly to ensure that your teens are emotionally healthy and happy at school, let your teens know in advance you will be looking to hear:

- At least one specific socially focused story.
    - About a sporting event or concert they attended;
    - Going for ice cream or coffee with a classmate;
    - A sorority or fraternity activity.
- At least one specific academically focused story.
    - Who's (are) their favorite professor (s) and why?
    - A paper they are working on
    - What steps they have taken on developing their resumes and/or progressing in their internship search.
- If the student plays an instrument, or is involved in sports or the theater, this is another topic about which you should get an update. This is not an opportunity to ask if they are practicing as much as they should. Remember you are now their coach and not their Supervisor. You could, however, inquire if your

young musician has a new favorite piece of music he/she is working on.

The purpose of the weekly call is for you to keep in touch, establish or reinforce your new role as Trusted Advisor AND to gain optics into any major problems, such as signs of emotional trouble. This is not an opportunity for you to solve problems.

This is a great opportunity for teens to learn the art of conversation, if they haven't already. Maintaining a conversation and expressing interest in others is a skill that they will need as they enter the workforce.

What You Should Share

Keep it short but be prepared to share something that happened since the last time you spoke.
- Is there a project you've been working on that you are proud of?
- Is there a pesky co-worker who has been exceptionally annoying recently?
- Did the dog do something particularly funny this week?
- Do you have a shared hobby or interest (theatre, music, other) you could discuss?
- Discuss a recent sporting event.
- Discuss your views on current affairs/politics.
- Share your thoughts on a recent movie or TV show you have seen.
- Perhaps you are planning a joint trip at the end of the school year. Share whatever information you've found about your destination.

Be sure to keep your comments lighthearted. This is not the time to share major challenges in your life. While it is important to keep the conversation real—as this helps to transition the relationship to one more of peers— you should not cause your teen to worry while not at home with you and with limited ability to help.

Contract

If necessary, come up with a contract before your teen leaves. You will know if you need this. If you suspect you will need a contract in place to ensure your teen communicates, it's OK to go ahead and attach his/her allowance to it. This may seem harsh but the reality is that depression on college campuses runs high and while you want your teen to develop resources to solve problems on his/her own, you are still parenting, and if there is a real problem brewing, knowing earlier is better than when there is a serious problem. Also be clear that there will be consequences if he/she doesn't maintain the communication plan. And be prepared to follow through. The consequences include your making an impromptu trip to the campus to see for yourself that your son or daughter is physically and emotionally healthy.

Finally, on the topic of a communication plan, there are likely many family members who have been supporting your teen leading up to college who will be excited about your child's success. This group might include aunts, uncles, grandparents, and cousins. It might also include some mentors. A very effective way for your teen to demonstrate gratitude for their support along the way is to send a group e-mail once a semester. In addition to allowing others to feel appreciated you increase the chances of them keeping your teen in mind. This may result in extra prayers, a card with $20 in it, or they might be on the lookout for a way to assist your teen in expanding his/her network when the time comes to seek an internship, employment or other connection.

Sample paragraphs for your teen to include in the group email:

(1) I can't believe the school year is almost over. It's been a great year. Want to update you on my classes, internship, upcoming travel and/or other summer plans.
(2) My favorite class or professor this semester was….(and why).
(3) Upcoming internship, why I am excited. What I hope to learn.
(4) Summer travel. Who I am going with? The name of my trip. What cities I will be visiting. I am (or am not) staying with a host family.
(5) Looking forward to time with my family this summer. What I've missed most is…
(6) Conclusion: Thankful for support from family and the opportunity to attend such a great school.

Communicating/Teamwork

The Benefits of a Student with Excellent Communication Skills

When Russell was on a college tour at one of the top Engineering programs in the United States, he and a group of other prospective students were placed in a room and told to wait for an administrator to come in. After waiting a while, Russell went to the front of the room and declared that they may as well introduce themselves and get to know one another. As it happens, the administrators were looking through a two-way mirror and were so impressed with his initiative and social ease that they offered him admission before he left.

In his first semester he ran into some problems. He and his high school girlfriend broke up and there were a lot of other adjustments that led to his grades being just okay. One thing he did continue to improve on were his social skills by participating in acting classes. During his sophomore year he followed his passion and spent the fall participating in a number of hackathons sponsored by the large companies that typically hired people from his school. A hackathon is an event, typically lasting several days, in which a large number of people meet to engage in collaborative computer programming. He won or came in second place in a number of categories. The combination of his success at the hackathons and his ability to communicate and engage others really set him apart. This ability was rewarded by his ability to, after many rounds of interviews, win a coveted internship at Microsoft. One of his classmates, who was a top student, approached him a month after everyone knew where they would be spending the summer and said to Russell, "I should have that internship at Microsoft. I am a better student." His classmate was disappointed, but he also realized that he was at a disadvantage because of his lack of communication skills.

Being an effective communicator means that you know how to get your point across to whomever your audience may be. It also means recognizing that we are ALL salespeople. The sooner we recognize how important this skill is, the more quickly we can hone our skills. Before you think to yourself, "This doesn't apply to me. I'm not going to be a salesperson," stop and recognize that you are one already. The question is whether or not you are an effective salesperson. Did you ever sell someone on the idea of cleaning the kitchen or mowing the lawn? Did you ever sell an idea at work? Have you sold your spouse or significant other on the idea of taking you out to dinner? Are you convinced yet that you are a sales person?

In addition to being an effective communicator, it is critical to be a good teammate. In many job postings for manager or other senior positions there is a requirement to 'manage across the matrix.' One of the core elements to success in managing across the matrix is being a good teammate. Managing across the matrix means you have to know how to work outside of your own department to get things done. This is especially tricky in a leadership position when you often need to incentivize people with whom you don't work to do the work you want them to. Your teen is a long way from management, but understanding how this works will prove to be important. For example, as a student, he/she will be called upon to work on group projects while in college.

Perhaps you have heard of Adam Grant. Mr. Grant is a highly regarded professor at the esteemed Wharton Business School in Philadelphia. His book Give and Take describes just how different things are today than they have been traditionally in terms of achieving success. Traditionally, we focused on the individual drivers of success: passion, hard work, talent, and luck. What's different today is that success is much more dependent upon how we interact with others. This is a huge shift in thinking.

Grant notes that at work most people operate as takers, matchers, or givers. Takers are defined as those who strive to get as much as possible from others; a matcher's goal is to trade evenly; and givers are the rare breed of people who contribute to assist others without expecting anything in return.

What professor Grant describes in his book is just how big an impact these three archetypes have on success. Simply put, some givers get exploited and burn out, but the rest achieve extraordinary results across a wide range of industries. Grant includes wonderful stories to illustrate this point across a number of industries and even in sports. . Perhaps you will consider giving yourself the gift of reading Mr. Grant's book.

The Thank You Letter

Once students begin to look for a job, one of the things that will set them apart or keep them in consideration is whether or not they have remembered to send a thank you note. It is something that many have fallen out of the habit of doing.

Channeling Emily Post, people always appreciate a thank you note. Handwritten notes are warmer and more personal than a phone call or email, and only second best to thanking someone in person. Email is great when you just need to say a simple thanks quickly. Some of the times that a thank you note would be appropriate for your teen to send are:
- After a job interview
- To someone who has written a letter of recommendation
- At the end of an internship
- Upon receipt of a care package while at school.

Not only is it just good manners, there is a somewhat selfish reason as well. When you acknowledge someone and appreciate them, they are more apt to do it again. Look for a link to the tool we use in our family to make it easier to write a letter www.pleasedontcomehome.com.

Presidential Level Communication Skills

Successful people are generally at ease communicating their thoughts to others. Consider politics. Regardless of your political party you can admire the communication skills of our United States Presidents. The three that come to mind immediately as standouts are: Barack Obama, Bill Clinton and Ronald Reagan. Their above average ability to connect and communicate not only aided them in becoming President, but also helped them consistently to achieve their goals. In fact, Ronald Reagan was so skilled at getting his point across he had the nickname The Great Communicator.

Millennials

Millennials have unique challenges. They have grown up with Smartphones and are so accustomed to texting, tweeting, Instagramming, and Snapchatting with friends and family that they often lack basic communication skills. I recall that for my daughter's 13th birthday celebration I took a group of eight teens out for dinner. We went to a restaurant that was fancy enough for the teens to get dressed up a bit with the girls in dresses and the few boys who attended in button down shirts. I sat at a separate table with a friend I had invited to join us. Imagine my surprise when I walked over to the teen table and every one of them was on their cell phones. It seemed that the only way they knew how to communicate was via their cell phones!

Recently, a survey of employers conducted by *The Chronicle of Higher Education* and *American Public Media's Marketplace* found that:

"When it comes to the skills most needed by employers, job candidates are lacking most in written and oral communication skills, adaptability and managing multiple priorities, and making decisions and problem solving."

How is this even possible? This generation is more intertwined in ways unlike any previous generation. And they communicate constantly with one another. How could they be so bad at communicating with others? Experts have developed a wide range of theories to explain this. To be honest, the why really isn't important. Whatever the cause, it is Millennials' communication skills (or lack thereof) that often hamper their professional aspirations. What is important is that they will need communication skills for any career path they choose.

It's Not Just What You Say But How You Say It

One of the first things to note about communicating is that we communicate in three different modalities and that what you say is NOT always the most important thing in getting your point across.

Dr. Albert Mehrabian a Psychology professor at UCLA conducted a study on communication. He arrived at two conclusions. His study demonstrates that there are three elements in any face-to-face communication: The words you use, the tone of your voice and your non-verbal communication (body language). Further his study proved that your body language is particularly important for communicating feelings and attitude, especially when they are incongruent. In other words, if words disagree with your tone of voice and body language, people tend to believe the tonality and body language.

Non-verbal communication of body language can include any of the following elements: posture (e.g. slouching), appearance (e.g. untidiness), head movements (e.g. nodding), hand movements (e.g. waving), eye movements (e.g. winking), facial expressions (e.g. frown), body contact (e.g. shaking hands) and closeness (e.g. invading someone's space)

Dr. Mehrabian validated that receivers of communication assign the following percentages to the credibility based upon:

> 55 percent of their weight to the speaker's body language;
> 38 percent to the tone and music of their voice;
> 7 percent to their words.

Effective communication is an important skill that you will want your emerging young adults to be adept at. Help get them started by introducing the following two important and simple rules:

- Look into the eyes of the person with whom you are communicating. This means don't look at your phone, don't look at the floor or off into the distance.
- You must be able to communicate verbally as opposed to sending a text message.

Building Communication Skills

Toastmasters	The environment in a Toastmasters club is friendly and supportive. Toastmasters strive to ensure that at each meeting, whether you are a complete beginner or an advanced speaker, you know that you are welcome. You aren't required to speak at each club meeting. Those speaking either practice giving prepared speeches or brief impromptu presentations, known as Table Topics. There is also the opportunity serve in other roles such as timekeeper. There is no rush and no pressure: The Toastmasters program allows you to progress at your own pace. Joining Toastmasters is relatively low cost and is an excellent investment of time and money.
Speech Class in College	This option offers valuable instruction and feedback from an expert.
Leadership Role in a Club	This is a great way to get regular practice speaking to a group. Depending on your role you might be called upon to share the minutes from a previous meeting, share the status of a project in progress or to kick off the meeting with a humorous story.

8

Celebrate

"Commitment is what transforms promise to reality."

Abraham Lincoln
16th President of the United States

We've come a long way! If I have successfully fulfilled my mission, I hope that you feel inspired and prepared to step into a new role as Trusted Advisor, and are equipped to transition to a new relationship with your college bound young adults. In this new and exciting chapter, you will continue to make a difference in their lives, if you choose to. Your advice, experience and skills are just what you need to enter the next phase of parenting.

You can do this! As you step into this new role you will see your young adult mature and grow into an independent person. It won't happen over night, but with your consistent love and support as a Trusted Advisor it will happen. Parenting is the greatest gift and challenge we will ever face and you've got this!

I applaud you for your investment in yourself and your young adult. Please be sure to share and celebrate your success on the book's website or Facebook page. If you run into up-and-coming parents about to transition into this new role please give them this book or share what you've learned.

I feel honored that our paths have crossed and that I've been able to share what I've learned. I'm still learning! Experts are always students first. It's been a great joy writing this book for you and our community of parents with college bound teens.

Regardless, of how you ended up with this book I know that you continued to read because you are one of the amazing and committed parents who wants to make a difference in this world by sending out talented, contributing and independent young adults. If that is true, I'd like to share one more story before saying farewell for now.

From Suffering to Powerful

Manny is a divorced and remarried father of two college-aged daughters. When his oldest daughter, Cristina, was entering what should have been her senior year in college she discovered that she would not be able to graduate on time because she had neglected to take two classes required for her major. So, she would need to return to campus the following year and complete the required classes. Cristina figured since she would be attending school, she would take a full class load and continue to live in the apartment that she and her sister, Maria, who was entering her junior year at the same school, had rented the previous school year. When her father probed as to how she could have made such an error in planning and questioned how she planned to pay her expenses she was resentful and said she just assumed that he would continue to pay.

As you can imagine, he was not happy. In fact, he was angry and suffering with the thought of how this would impact his finances. He had not budgeted to pay for an extra semester at school or her living costs. After having two children in college for the previous two years he was looking forward to getting a start on directing his discretionary income to his retirement. His own parents had started a family much younger than he did. His dad was twenty-five years old when Manny was born. Manny was thirty-five years old when his first daughter was born. He saved some money for college but with the expense of his divorce from the girls' mother he hadn't saved as much as planned. And, unlike, his parents who had twenty years more to work by the time he graduated college, he would only have another ten years to work and continue to build his retirement fund once his daughters had completed their education.

He was also feeling very frustrated at Cristina's dismissive attitude. He had always enjoyed a close relationship with both of his daughters, even during and after the divorce. He realized then that with the limited communication between him and his ex wife, he just assumed that she was overseeing more of the girls' activities and providing guidance to them in some of life's basics.

After he calmed down he talked with Cristina and discovered that she didn't even know how to write a check. She didn't know how to read a lease for an apartment or a car. She didn't know how to apply for a credit card with a competitive bank rate. She didn't know how to balance her bank account, or open utilities in her name. In short, she didn't know any of what he considered the basics.

Manny and I talked and I reminded him that he had the power to turn things around. He could bring all of the creativity and resourcefulness that he brought to his career to empower his daughters and save himself some money, and some stress.

Over the summer he harnessed his power and developed a plan for addressing his two daughters' attitudes and their lack of knowledge. First, he had a heart to heart with both girls and took responsibility for his part in their lack of concern about the extra expenses, and their lack of basic knowledge. Next, he developed his own curriculum that each girl was required to complete and use before he would deposit funds for the next semester's expenses.

The coursework totaled about eighty hours. He got very resourceful and used as much free and available information as he could. He leveraged YouTube videos, contacted his bank and tapped into their resources and educational materials. He turned off the electricity that had been in his name in their shared apartment and instructed Cristina to figure out how to get new service started in her name. Maria was required to arrange for Internet and cable service in the apartment.

Next up, Manny instructed each girl to develop a game plan to share with him. He informed Maria that she would need to map out her planned courses for the next two years and then have it reviewed by an administrator at her school. Cristina also needed to write down her plan for what she would be doing after college to provide for her expenses if she had not yet landed a more permanent job.

Additionally, he required each of his daughters to work over the summer and to save $500 so that they could contribute to the cost of their schoolbooks. The intent of this was not to save him $1,000, but for each of his daughters to have something invested in their college costs since he was paying tuition, room and board. He also, deposited funds in their account to pay the electricity for the year.

At first, Cristina and Maria weren't very happy with dad. They were very comfortable with him taking care of everything. If they needed money, they called him or mom. If they needed something fixed in their apartment they called him. And they didn't like the idea of having to study over the summer. But once they returned to school in the fall they actually felt a bit more empowered. They also, started to think a bit more about how they spent money. It didn't take them long to realize that if they remembered to turn off the lights when they went out they might not have to spend the entire amount that Manny provided for electricity to the electric company. They could put that money towards other things that they would love to do or have.

In the final analysis, Manny felt relieved that he would be able to avoid Maria making similar mistakes in her class choices. Additionally, he enjoyed seeing his daughters begin to mature, and the positive changes in his relationship with them.

Remember to Love them, Lead them and Let them fly.

9
Bonus

"Trust yourself. Create the kind of self that you will be happy to live with all your life. Make the most of yourself by fanning the tiny, inner sparks of possibility into flames of achievement."

Golda Meir
Prime Minister of Israel

DO YOU!

Today's youth have an expression that is valuable for parents with a student off to college to adopt. "I'm going to do me and you do you". For the last 18 years, as parents we have lovingly and devotedly cared for these precious beings, and the reward is that now we get to turn our attention back to ourselves. It's time to celebrate and acknowledge us for a job well done. So stick your arm in the air, bend at the elbow and pat yourself on the back.

Wheel of You

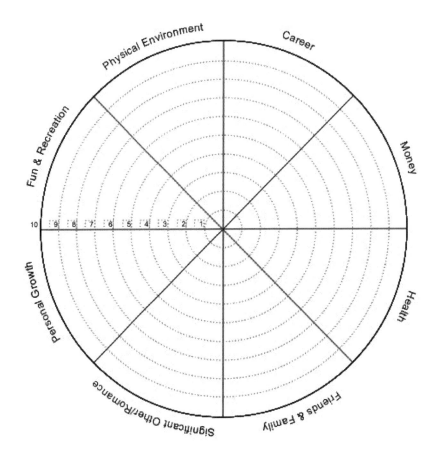

See the website (www.pleasedontcomehome.com) to download your wheel and directions on how to determine where you are, where you want to go, and how to get there.

It's time to check in. After years of taking care of your child you now have some time to think about you. Even if you have other children at home it is likely that you have at least a little more time in your schedule and perhaps you have a lot more time. Either way it is time to put the focus on you.

For some of us it's been so long that we might not even know how to accomplish this. When you think about it, for the last eighteen years there has been little opportunity to do anything that didn't require you to consider your children. In the beginning it was caring for all of their needs from diaper changes to making bottles. As they got older what they needed likely changed, but nonetheless, they still needed you.

I am reminded of a colleague I had when my girls were two and four. She had recently decided to work part time. When asked about her decision to do this she shared that her two daughters were ages twelve and fourteen and that they needed her more now than they did when they were two and four. Frankly, this comment really scared me. At the time I was working so hard to balance the needs and desires of my children, a demanding husband and a large team at work. "What more could I give?" I thought to myself. And if I was being honest, I thought that by the time they could do more for themselves, I would surely be ready for a much-needed break. I mean really, how could I keep up this pace for the next ten+ years?

The truth of the matter is that you have to make taking care of yourself a priority. Remember the lesson the airlines teach us: In case of emergency, put your air mask on before you can assist someone traveling with you. Effective parenting works the same way. When you make time for yourself you will be able to give more to those around you.

Fortunately, over the years I learned and implemented some tools that allowed me to gain balance in my life. More than that, it allowed me to not only get through raising my daughters but also to enjoy the process as a single parent.

So, even if you still have children at home, now is the time to shift some focus back to you!

If someone were to ask you for directions to the Statue of Liberty, what is the thing you would need to know first to assist them? Well, you would need to know where you are starting from to be able to direct that person, wouldn't you? The Wheel of You represents the starting point. Where are you today?

The first step is to assess where you are in eight principle areas of life. This is not a statement of how much of something you have (like money) but your level of satisfaction in a given area. Print your own copy of the Wheel of You from the website (www.pleasedontcomehome.com) and assess your life in each area.

Topic 1: Family & Friends

There are two components to see how you rate on this section of the wheel.

Do you have the relationships that you would like with your family and friends? These are your non-intimate relationships: your neighbors, friends from your religious affiliation, and your friends from college or work.

Are these relationships in good shape or just tolerable? Do you have time to spend nurturing these relationships? Do you strive to make time for these people in your life? Do you make it a priority to support and spend time with the people closest to you?

Assign yourself a score between 0 and 10 and then fill in the wheel accordingly.

Topic 2: Significant Other/Romance

Our intimate relationships can range from "not in one (and don't want to be)", to "in a relationship, planning my way out," to "have roommates," or hopefully "in a passionate and loving relationship."   If you aren't in a relationship give yourself 0 and if you are in a passionate and loving relationship give yourself 10.

Topic 3: Fun/Recreation Hobbies

About ten years ago as a single mom living in Chicago, I decided that I really needed to carve out some time for me. I realized that there could be an important lesson in this for my girls too. I was showing them that although I was their mom, it was okay for me to:
- take time for myself;
- continue to learn;
- and that while I worked hard at my career to take care of them it was important for me to have fun too.

I decided to learn salsa. There was something about the beauty and confidence in the way I saw the ladies being twirled around the dance floor that appealed to me. I decided that I was going to become proficient. I didn't know how I was going to do it. I just decided that it was important to me and that I would figure it out. In fact, I set a goal of twelve months to becoming good enough to go to any party or club and be a sought after partner.

Once I set the goal, I broke the goal down to bite size pieces. The first step was to get lessons! I found a local Latin dance studio and got started with my first lesson. It was exhilarating and fun, and I knew immediately that I had found the right new hobby for me. Sometimes it just takes that first step. Or in the case of the cha cha, one step backwards and three steps forward.

Do you have a hobby or have you given it up to take care of your children? If you have forgotten, or put your hobby aside, it's time to remember those things that you loved to do and resurrect them!. What do you do for fun? How satisfied are you that you have something you do for fun and that you have sufficient time to pursue it? Assign yourself a score between 0 and 10 and then fill in the wheel accordingly.

Topic 4: Physical Vitality/Self Care

There's a saying about being the richest man in the graveyard. Are you in good physical shape? This is not simply a question of whether or not you are carrying extra weight. This is about vitality. Do you have the energy to do all of the things you want to accomplish or are you too tired to enjoy your life?

Self care – do you take time for yourself? As parents we are often on a treadmill to take care of our families. And if you add work to this, your time commitments may seem never ending. Some of you are thinking, "When would I even have time to for myself?" The truth is very simple. You have to make it a priority. And by doing so there is a lesson for your children. Consider the time you devote to your own self-care and assign yourself a score between 0 and 10 and then fill in the wheel accordingly.

Topic 5: Finances

When sending your child off to college this could be a loaded subject! – Either you have successfully saved sufficient funds for your child's education and the next four years won't be significantly financially stressful for you, or you haven't saved enough and are worrying about how to pay for (or make a financial contribution to) your child's education. More importantly, how is your retirement nest egg looking? Go ahead and give yourself a score based on how satisfied you are with your current financial state, and then fill in the wheel accordingly.

Topic 6: Personal Growth/Spirituality

In 2004 my life was looking very different than it is today. I had recently lost my mom who was my best friend and shortly thereafter my husband and I divorced. Things were moving forward in my life, but they weren't great. Frankly, it was a pretty stinky place to be. It was then that I began a deep dive into the personal growth space. I took a hard look at the different areas in my life and committed to making improvements. In eight years I tripled my spendable income, met and married the man of my dreams, and increased my health and energy. Whether or not these are goals of yours, what I know for sure is, if you don't grow you die. Are you continuing to develop and grow? Assign yourself a score between 0 and 10 and then fill in the wheel accordingly.

Topic 7: Physical Environment

Do you live in the home or region that you desire? My husband had a colleague who lived in Maryland. One winter she decided she had had enough with the snow. So she packed up her husband and kids and moved to Hawaii. All that winter I enjoyed seeing posts on Facebook of her and her family surfing while we were freezing in the winter snow. She made a massive shift in her physical environment. That might not be for everyone. Perhaps a new couch could bring immense satisfaction. Remember this is about what you want. How much joy are you getting from your physical environment? Assign yourself a score between 0 and 10 and then fill in the wheel accordingly.

Topic 8: Career/Mission

How is your career or mission coming along? Wait, what do I mean by mission? Whether you've had a paying career outside of the home or not, your mission is that thing that drives you. It may align with your career or it may not. Your mission is something bigger than you are.

My mission is to impact the world by helping parents promote the development of independent, successful and happy young adults. This calling was so great that I resigned from my employer of 20 years to focus all of my attention on writing and publishing this book. As you move through life your mission may change. For many years mine was to raise great kids.

You may be thinking, "My mission has been to raise this child to be a productive member of society. Great! What's next?

For those with careers outside the home, is it time to go into overdrive in your career? Do you even know what's next for you in this space? Do you have professional goals? Are you on track with achieving these goals? What is your level of satisfaction in this area of your life?

If you have been home with your children until now, is there an organization that you want to devote your energy toward? Do you have some expertise you want to share in the form of a book or video series?

Assign yourself a score between 0 and 10 and then fill in the wheel accordingly.

When you are done you will have something that looks like this:

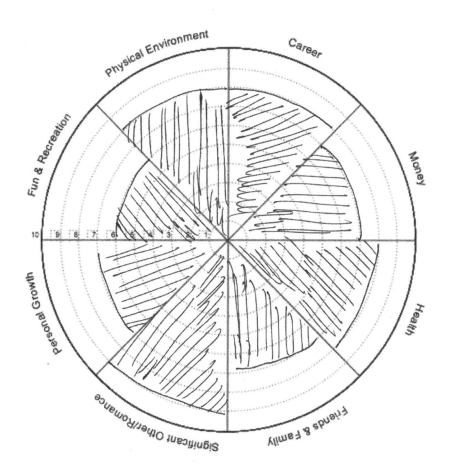

Imagine if this circle represented a tire on a car you were driving down the road called life. How smooth or bumpy would your ride be?

You have just completed the first step in 'Doing You'. Outstanding! It's time to celebrate! Go ahead and give yourself a round of applause. This is a huge accomplishment, as you are way ahead of most people who are just going through life with no ownership of what happens to them in life.

Join the Discussion

Go to the website below to join a group of parents, grandparents, mentors and guardians who are striving to create independent young adults.

Visit this page today:

www.pleasedontcomehome.com/discussion

Acknowledgements

I feel very grateful for the twists and turns my life has taken to end up at this place. I believe that I have been divinely guided.

This book is dedicated to my parents, Russell and Gayle Hawkins. Mom, we lost you too soon but I am thankful every day that I had such an amazing mother and role model. I couldn't have designed a more supportive and supportive person if I had been given a magic wand. I am continually thankful for my father and his wife Virginia for their support in raising my girls as a single parent over the years.

To my hero and protector, Jose. It is no understatement to say that I would not be completing this book without your love and support. You always believe in my gifts and talents and push me when needed. I feel incredibly fortunate that our paths crossed. You are a wonderfully supportive, hilarious, kind, savvy, talented and giving soul. I am humbled by the love we have for one another and life we are creating.

I must, of course, thank my daughters who are great cheerleaders in my efforts. I couldn't have asked for two better daughters. You have tested and tried me over the years and stretched my parenting patience and skills. You are both beautiful and caring souls. I love watching you share your gifts with the world. I am also thankful for my two bonus daughters, Amanda and Cristina. I love watching the two of you leave college and independently build your future.

My brother and sister, Russell and Cynthia Hawkins, are the two people who support me always. One of the first lessons our mother taught us was to love our siblings and always have one another's back. We have passed this lesson on to our own children. They not only cheer me on but also are the quickest to kick me in the butt if that is what is needed. With them as siblings there was no chance I was going to embarrass myself on American Idol.

My Aunt Izetta and cousin Regina Jackson have been my parenting guides after losing my mom so early. In my most challenging times they were there to get me back on the right path.

This book would not have been complete without the incredible skill and patience of my editor, Gayle Wiegand. Your commitment to my mission was so appreciated. And your enthusiasm made this process all the more enjoyable.

What can I say about Alex Changho, who has provided the marketing talent to help me get this message out to parents? You are inspirational with your energy and zeal. Thanks for driving the process of getting this book up on Amazon so I could focus on the message.

I am fortunate enough to call a group of women part of my inner circle. They didn't so much help me with the book but they always believe in me and can be called upon at a moment's notice for support or counsel. Thank you Lorrie King, Kathryn Badger and Linda Couch.

If you are not part of a mastermind start one today! For several years I have had the counsel and support of an incredibly talented group of women. We have laughed and shared tears and encouraged one another to pursue our dreams. Thank you Fabienne Meuleman, Courtney Minor Monson, Valeria Grunbaum, and Lisa Lea Cooney.

There are other friends who pitched in on this effort as well. They believed in the message or me and lent their expertise. Thank you Heidi Martin for reading each unedited chapter as I wrote and providing your invaluable feedback! And thanks Celeste Lee and Lorrie King for your counsel on selecting a title for my book!

To my friends and former co-workers at IBM thank you for being so exemplary and for teaching me every day about business and professionalism. That you live IBM's core values every day makes the world a better place. IBM's three core values are: Dedication to every client's success; Innovation that matters, for our company and for the world; Trust and personal responsibility in all relationships.

In 2004, I purchased a set of CD's from Anthony Robbins. Who knew the impact that decision would have on my life. Thanks Tony and Sage Robbins for leading me home to my core and encouraging me to recognize my gifts. It has been an incredible journey and I am honored to serve as part of your leadership team to enable others to reach their goals. It is not just the lessons you have taught but also the incredible community of caring souls you built that makes my life just a bit brighter.

Big shout out to Brendon Burchard whose guidance has been truly transformational as he provided a framework for how to get my message out to the world.

Finally, my current and future peers in parenting – I am honored to be among you. We are and continue to do the most important job we will ever have. Keep on keeping on!

About Allyson Hawkins Ward

Allyson Hawkins Ward has come a long way since her days as a single mother of two, struggling to make ends meet and to balance the demands of a big corporate career and the love and care of her daughters. Through her dedicated focus and a deep desire to help others find success, Allyson has emerged as a highly regarded, multi-faceted business executive.

In her over twenty year career she developed her sales and marketing skills, earning high reviews from her management team, peers and staff. Her commitment to her clients and driving revenue for the company earned her admittance to IBM's prestigious 100% Club. Additionally, she has been recognized as a passionate leader advocating for her team's success both professionally and personally.

Over the past 15 years Allyson pursued a deep dive of study with Anthony Robbins in the areas of personal development, leadership and business mastery and now serves as part of the leadership team as a Trainer at live events. She has completed coaching coursework with CTI and Organizational Development.

Allyson has accomplished all of this while maintaining a family-friendly lifestyle. And now leads programs geared towards working parents to lead their children to independence, excelling in the workplace and gaining more joy in life.

She resides in Maryland with her husband, José, and the last of their four children.

Made in the USA
Middletown, DE
28 July 2016